T0030537

A SYNTHESIZING MIND

A SYNTHESIZING MIND

A Memoir from the Creator of Multiple Intelligences Theory

HOWARD GARDNER

The MIT Press
Cambridge, Massachusetts
London, England

This book was set in Scala and ScalaSans by New Best-set Typesetters Ltd. Printed and bound in the United States of America.

Library of Congress Cataloging-in-Publication Data

Names: Gardner, Howard, 1943– author.
Title: A synthesizing mind : a memoir from the creator of multiple
    intelligences theory / Howard Gardner.
Description: Cambridge, Massachusetts : The MIT Press, [2020] | Includes
    bibliographical references and index.
Identifiers: LCCN 2019055253 | ISBN 9780262044264 (hardcover)
Subjects: LCSH: Gardner, Howard, 1943– | Psychologists—Biography. |
    Multiple intelligences.
Classification: LCC BF109.G367 A3 2020 | DDC 150.92 [B]—dc23
LC record available at https://lccn.loc.gov/2019055253

10 9 8 7 6 5 4 3 2

To my mentors, who taught me so much

To my tor-mentors, who demonstrated what I should not do or be

To my students (and grand-students), who continue to teach me

To public radio, whose news and classical music have sustained me for decades

To my family, whose love has sustained me throughout my life

CONTENTS

CONTENTS

INTRODUCTION

I knew things were different as soon as I walked into the room.

It was the fall of 1984, and I'd been invited by the National Association of Independent Schools to speak at its annual conference. The venue was the Hilton Hotel in midtown Manhattan. I had been asked to speak about my recently published book, *Frames of Mind: The Theory of Multiple Intelligences.*

A researcher and occasional teacher in psychology, I was already an experienced lecturer. I had written many scholarly and popular articles, a number of books and textbooks, and had even won some awards. My new book had gotten considerable attention and I had already given a few talks on the topic, both before and after the book's publication date in September 1983.

As I made my way down the hallway and into the lecture hall, I noted that the room was completely filled, even overflowing. And as soon as I walked in, the pre-lecture buzz abruptly ceased. In the suddenly hushed environment, I observed people gesturing toward me as the chatter gradually resumed at a much lower volume. When I was introduced, I was met by a round of applause, unusual in academic settings at that time. During the lecture, many in the audience seemed held in rapt attention, much more so than at standard conference talks where wandering to and fro and shuffling papers audibly are the norm. And after the talk, I was asked to sign *a lot* of books (this was decades before the advent of the "selfie" or the Kindle).

My intimation was correct. The publication of a book about the theory of multiple intelligences had changed my life forever. Before, I had been a research psychologist plying my trade; now, I was the author of a much-discussed treatise and the creator of a controversial theory. I had written several works of synthesis that were principally about *other* people's ideas; now my *own* ideas had become the subject of praise, criticism, and debate. And while I preferred (and still prefer!) not to be recognized on the street or at the airport, I gradually got used to the idea of assenting when asked if I were, indeed, "Howard Gardner," or "Dr. Gardner," or "Professor Gardner," or even "*the* Howard Gardner."

In some ways, I found my notoriety as a scholar and budding public intellectual satisfying. Though I don't think I had dreamed before about being a minor celebrity—that's not my inclination—it is admittedly gratifying to be known, to be invited to interesting conferences and parties in evocative settings, and to increase one's nonsalaried income. In this book, I touch on some of these rewards.

However, my primary motives for writing a memoir are different, and twofold.

First, in our time, and especially in the United States, speakers and writers come to be associated with a particular idea. I have written thirty books and hundreds of articles, and have carried out dozens of research studies, but I am known—and concede that in all likelihood I will *always* be known—as the creator or "father" of multiple intelligences (MI). In no way do I renounce or regret having developed this theory. Indeed, I have spent some time working on it in the decades since I first introduced the ideas. Yet, by personality, temperament, and calling, I have never wanted to continue working only on MI ideas. I have in fact resented the contention that, just because I developed the theory, I am obligated to keep refining it and, even less alluringly, to keep defending it. Life is short. I have many other ideas and interests, and I deserve the option of turning my attention to them and not remaining a captive of MI theory.

Also, while the idea of multiple intelligences has caught the attention of many individuals all over the world, there is no guarantee that they have understood the theory. And, alas, my innumerable efforts over the years to discourage misunderstandings have not been notably successful. Moreover, while I rarely question the motives of those who wave the MI banner, they have sometimes deployed or refashioned the ideas in destructive ways. In fact, as detailed later in this book, the misuse in one case was so blatant that I had to denounce that abuse publicly, and that unhappy event has radically changed the course of my work in the ensuing decades. Largely as a consequence of that distortion of my ideas, I stopped being a psychologist investigating human cognition, and I began an effort—now over a quarter of a century old—to understand and promote the ethical use of whatever intellectual and creative strengths we have.

In this book, I trace the origin of my ideas and themes in my personal history; their development in the early years of my research; the initial reception of MI theory; and the zigs and zags, both scholarly and cultural, I have taken in the four decades since I began to develop the theory.

But I have another, perhaps less predictable but to my mind more pressing, motivation for offering this book. For most of my scholarly and writing life, I have focused on human minds in general or, to put it differently, on the minds of our species. In what follows, I seek to examine *my own mind*—the mind that produced the theory of multiple intelligences and various other scholarly concepts over a half century. To my surprise, it is *not* a kind of mind that is easily or readily explained in terms of MI theory.

To get to the nub of the matter: I am convinced that my own mind is *a synthesizing mind*. The motivation to synthesize and the ability to synthesize have to do with one's overarching goals; and the act of synthesizing can draw on various intelligences, and combinations of intelligences, in various ways. In dissecting the act, or art, of synthesis, I believe that I can illuminate a kind of mind that has not been much analyzed and that may prove especially important in the chapter of human history that lies ahead.

From the very beginning of my studies, I have been attracted to a certain approach to research and writing. Technically, one could call it "qualitative social science," but it's more accurate, and less pretentious, to call this approach "works of synthesis" about the human mind, human nature, and human culture. This is what I have admired since my early school days; what my mentors— ranging from psychoanalyst Erik Erikson to sociologist David Riesman to psychologist Jerome (Jerry) Bruner—modeled for me; what my high school hero, American historian Richard Hofstadter, and my college hero, cultural critic Edmund Wilson, accomplished so arrestingly and evocatively in their writings; and it's fundamentally what I've tried to do in just about all of my writing and particularly in *Frames of Mind*.

I believe that the kind of work in which I have long been engaged, situated between journalism on the one hand and experimental laboratory science on the other, is a valid and particularly precious (and possibly particularly precarious) form of knowledge. It's what I do and what I think I am good at—my comparative strength, so to speak. And yet, I am concerned that such works of synthesis may be on the wane. Alas, the trend in the academy is toward an ever sharper focus on highly technical quantitative work within standard disciplinary boundaries. A corresponding trend in the media is toward the single and simple "big idea," as well as toward commentators who can reliably produce the precise string of words desired by the interviewer, seemingly irrespective of the prompt. It would be most regrettable if the kind of ambitious synthesis of concepts or ideas that I admire, and that I have tried to create, were to disappear from the agora, from the public space.

And so, in what follows, I seek to describe, interpolate, and illuminate two themes that reflect these motivations: (1) to show what's involved in creating a new perspective on intelligence, in changing the "human conversation" about the intellect, and to illustrate my resistance to being held captive, seemingly forever, by that conversation changer; and (2) to investigate the kind of mind that creates a new concept about human experience and that, ever since childhood, has sought to synthesize vast amounts of information and capture the resulting synthesis in a form that makes sense to the creator, and can be conveyed clearly to a wider population.

I am clearly and candidly autobiographical when that advances my narrative and my argument, but this is not a "life and loves" narrative. It is, rather, an account of the life of a mind, a scholarly or intellectual memoir.

The story I relate unfolds in three parts.

In Part I, I describe the issues and factors that influenced the development of my mind as a child, a young student, and then a budding professional research psychologist and writer. Since I am the fashioner as well as the only subject of this narrative, I cannot know for sure *which* of the factors in my family, my hometown, my hobbies, interests, curiosities, strengths and weaknesses, friendships, activities, and choice of schools influenced me to become a synthesizer. But at the very least, I present a case study of the emergence of *one* synthesizing mind.

In Part II, I detail the emergence of the act of synthesizing for which I am best known, the theory of multiple intelligences. Then, proceeding from what I sensed that day when I spoke at the Hilton Hotel, I examine what happens when a perspective goes viral; my reactions both to scholarly criticism and to public approbation and appetites; the ways in which MI theory both "freed" me and "captured" me; and the various programs and projects developed by individuals influenced by MI theory, including those enterprises created by my colleagues and me.

In Part III, I unfold my myriad other research endeavors, seeking to discern how what may seem like scattered pursuits are linked by the capacities of a synthesizing mind. In an unexpected turn in my own scholarly life, the reaction to MI theory eventually led me to large-scale, decade-long studies of professional ethics and of higher education. Until the present essay, my work has concerned the generic human mind and the minds of prominent figures in the arts, sciences, and politics.

In the last chapters of this book, drawing on my own self-knowledge or "intrapersonal intelligence," I try at last to look in the mirror and figure out the operation of *my own synthesizing mind*: where it came from, how it works, what is distinctive about it, and what lessons this self-knowledge might yield for other persons with other minds in this and other times. I distinguish synthesizing from journalism, on the one hand, and from empirical social science, on the other. I also introduce a continuum of synthesizing: from the consensual conclusions in a standard textbook (I have written two myself) to the proposal of an original synthesis, as great scholars like biologist Darwin or historian Hofstadter have carried out, and as I have sought to do, far more modestly to be sure, in my studies of intelligences, creativity, and leadership.

Looking across my life's work, I try to demonstrate why the positing of powerful concepts, their exploration through wide and careful research, and their clear communication to both the scholarly community and the public is a worthwhile calling, one that we humans should continue to pursue and, indeed, to cherish as long as our species survives.

I

THE FORMATION OF A SYNTHESIZING MIND

MY TEN-YEAR-OLD MIND

If you had spied me at age ten, what might you have noticed? A somewhat plump but quite active youngster, with dark hair and thick glasses, probably with my nose buried deep in a book. Or slouching on a piano bench, playing a Bach prelude or fugue, often with my mother seated by my side. Or bent over a small portable typewriter, picking out words with two or three fingers, much as I am doing now on my laptop. What brought me to these childhood preoccupations?

My parents, Hilde Bella Weilheimer and Rudolf Gärtner, were born into comfortable middle-class Jewish families in Nuremberg, Germany. At surprisingly young ages for their time and social class—Hilde was twenty, Rudolf was twenty-three—they married and prepared for a conventional bourgeois life in the land where their families had prospered in recent generations.

The appointment of Adolf Hitler to the German chancellorship in January 1933 was a rude shock. Impressively forward-thinking, my parents moved to Milan in 1934, hoping to start a new life in Italy, sufficiently distant from the increasingly violent Nazi regime. But when it became clear that Italian leader Benito Mussolini shared Hitler's vision, one with no place for Jews, Hilde and Rudolf moved back to Germany. They had a child, Erich, born in September 1935. Thereafter, my parents' principal mission in life—and soon it became a matter *of* life—was to emigrate with Erich from Germany, preferably to the United States.

With Hilde and Erich essentially being held hostages by the already punitive Nazi regime, my father sailed three times to the United States. He was searching for someone, anyone, who would vouch for the three Gärtners and guarantee that the family would not become a financial burden on the United States. Success finally arrived in the summer of 1938 in the form of an affidavit from a school friend of my father who had relocated to California some years before.[1] The Gärtners assembled their possessions, paying four times the value of each item simply to take it with them to the United States, and boarded a ship to New York.

Knowing little English, with few friends or even acquaintances, and having to their name only $5.00 per person as allowed by the German authorities, the Gärtners arrived in New York on the night of November 9, 1938. That evening became infamous as Kristall-nacht, the night of broken glass. Hundreds of Jewish synagogues across Germany were damaged or destroyed and many Jews were

---

1. I recently learned that this friend, Alfred Marshütz, had to promise to guarantee their financial stability for five years.

arrested, injured, or even murdered, including some of my mother's close relatives.

But my parents were fortunate—fortunate to be German, rather than Eastern European (approximately three million Polish Jews were eventually killed by the Nazis and their sympathizers; close to 200,000 German Jews were killed); fortunate to have made it intact as a family to the United States; fortunate to be healthy and entrepreneurial.

But their good fortune did not last long. They moved from New York to Scranton, Pennsylvania—a small city of which they had never previously heard—and eked out a modest living. My father, who had never done any manual labor, carried oil tanks on his back for $15 a week. My mother, who had hitherto never cooked a meal or made a bed (even during the Depression, everyone in her social circle had maids), started a household that soon provided shelter for a variety of homeless refugees.

Then, in January 1943, tragedy struck. While sledding down a hill in Scranton, my brother Erich was diverted by a dog and ended up in a fatal accident. Many years later, my parents told me that had my mother not been three months pregnant with me, they would have killed themselves. From their point of view, *they had lost everything*—their home country, their occupations, many friends and members of their extended families, and now what was most precious to them, a very gifted young child. Even though Erich had not known three words of English upon his arrival in the States, he was so smart (a word that I heard a lot in English, German, and French) that he had been allowed to skip second grade.

In those days, rightly or wrongly, American parents were instructed to withhold bad news from their children. Therefore, rightly or wrongly, when in my presence, my parents never spoke about Germany, Hitler, the concentration camps, or their earlier lives. They were trying desperately to turn over a new leaf. Also, and perhaps more surprisingly, they never told me about Erich and his untimely death. When I saw and asked about framed photos of Erich around the house, I was informed that he was a boy who had "lived in the neighborhood." At one point, rifling through a drawer, I chanced upon some newspaper clippings about his death and any innocence abruptly ended. I use the phrase "any innocence" because children are far more observant and analytic than their parents realize. I think that at some level and in some way, despite the good intentions of baby expert Dr. Benjamin Spock and of my parents, I had known about both Erich Gärtner and Adolf Hitler.

I begin with these stories because these two events dominated or at the very least strongly colored my childhood, whether in spite of or perhaps on account of my parents' studied silence. Whereas most of my age-mates in northeastern Pennsylvania were second- or third-generation Americans, my sister Marion (born in 1946) and I came from a family where German was the native language (when my parents wanted to keep something secret they spoke in French or occasionally used Italian expressions); where German-speaking refugees were frequent visitors, dinner guests, or, all too often, occupants of the couches in our small third-floor walk-up apartment.

Needless to say, the Second World War and its aftermath (including the plights of many so-called displaced persons) were on everyone's mind in the late 1940s and into the 1950s. My father never really adapted to life in the United States. If he could have snapped his fingers and gone back to the Germany of the late 1920s, with its soccer matches, lager, and schnitzel, he would have gladly done so.

My mother, who lived with her mind intact until her death in 2013 at the age of 102, took the opposite approach. She adapted easily and well to the United States and never wanted to go near Germany again. (She was pleased that our family name was anglicized to Gardner.) But the specter of Erich's great promise and tragic demise was always on my parents' mind. Indeed, while I give both of my parents straight A's as parents, I knew—without knowing it—that I was the replacement child. Even my middle name, Earl, was a deliberate Americanized substitute for Eric(h). And continuing the commemoration, there have been several Eric(h)s in various branches of our family in subsequent generations.

Growing up in Germany, my parents were typical comfortable young people of the 1920s. They danced, partied, skied, and were quite social. But having lost a child in a sledding accident, they were very protective of me. They did not want me to be involved in any activity that might result in serious injury. I was essentially barred from any sports, never skied, never played tackle football. I did not ride a bicycle until I was in my twenties, long out of the family home, and have never felt fully comfortable on two wheels. I was not antisocial but, as seen in the opening cameo, my major activities were solitary—reading widely, writing regularly, and playing the piano assiduously. Even today, I prefer swimming to any team sports. I always had a few close friends and was reasonably social with those I knew well. But I was hardly gregarious, let alone the life of the party.

Instead, and I have realized this for decades, *I lived largely in my mind*. I played the piano nearly every day, thanks to a neighbor who noticed my musicality and gently pressured my parents to buy a piano—for $30. I also fooled around with an accordion and the organ at our temple, and eventually took up the flute in high school. I listened constantly to music of several genres on the radio, accumulated and listened to many records (mostly 33s rather than 45s or 78s), and no doubt heard music in my mind almost all of my waking hours, as I do to this minute. I read inveterately, whatever was available at home or in the Scranton public library, where I spent countless hours. I did not read simply to escape; I was curious about everything, from sports to the weather. I read a one-volume encyclopedia and kept the multivolume *World Book* next to my bed for easy reference. (Had I been born sixty years later, I would have kept search engines very busy.) I read many books in the highly popular "Landmark" series, but I was particularly fascinated by history and biography, two topics that revolved around human beings and the often-fateful choices that they make—or that are made for them. History and biography, chiefly of the period of the world wars, were also the subject of the few English language books at home, clearly reflecting my father's obsessions. And while I read stories, novels, and the magazine *Boys' Life*, I estimate that 80 percent of my reading was nonfiction.

In retrospect, I can say that I was reading widely and not particularly organizing what I had read in any conscious manner. But like many young people, I had a very keen memory, be it for historical or scientific or sports information. I drew on the information easily and made connections across areas—for example, comparing sports figures to historical figures, or media personalities to figures in contemporary politics, noting what was happening in two disparate societies or sectors during the same year. I suspect that I was also trying to understand the mysterious silences in my home, with respect to the death of my brother and the murder of millions of

Jews. Using language that I developed much later, I was seeing parallels, drawing connections, noting contrasts, making comparisons in a relatively *discipline-free* or *predisciplinary way*. My mind was like a vast collection of information floating around without any strong lines between the lanes. And since I had not yet studied formal disciplines like history, economics, or political science, I was making my own distinctions, comparisons, and connections.

And I loved to write. At age seven, with no prompts from anyone, I started a newspaper for my class. I had a small printing press at home, on whose platen I patiently placed every letter of every word, and then cranked the lever, painstakingly producing a four-page publication. I would be surprised if anyone, including my doting parents, ever read or retained a page of the newspaper. That did not matter! The pleasure was in writing things down. And all these years later that pleasure remains. As I type these words standing at my desk, I hope to send them out into the world. But I would continue to write, bearing witness to myself, even if the words were to disappear forever into the air or cyberspace.

And so, stepping back (or forth), if I were now to build a model of the development of a synthesizing mind—or at least a model that comes out of my own life—I would pick out these elements: exhibiting wide curiosity; assimilating and remembering mounds of facts and figures; raising questions but also attending carefully to answers, whether obtained from books, nature, mechanical experimentation, other persons, or one's own imagination; putting together these preliminary answers (in a nondisciplinary though not undisciplined manner) and seeing how they work—or don't work; and importantly, setting the answers down in some kind of symbolic system.

My mind was active day and night, often exhausting family and friends. In school, I was a good and easy student, finding myself invariably at the top of my class, and, though I don't relish writing these words, an expert test-taker. It was important for me to achieve in whichever activities I chose to focus on. We will never know whether I was as good a student or as easy a learner as my late, much cherished brother—but I suspect that at some level I was competing with him.

Did I have heroes? One clue comes from three photographs that hung in my bedroom during childhood. They were portraits by famed photographer Yousuf Karsh of physicist Albert Einstein and of novelist and short-story writer Ernest Hemingway, along with a Karsh-like photograph of my maternal grandfather, Martin Weilheimer, that still hang in my study today.[2] While I would not have so formulated it seventy years ago, they represented men who had achieved much in their respective domains of science, art, and business—and who set an expectation for me to do the same someday.

Thanks to another friend of the family, my parents were warned not to shelter me too much. And so, at age seven, I began to attend "sleep-away" camp. I hated it at first—being away from home, spending much of the day participating in competitive sports for which I had neither talent nor ardor—but over the course of seven years, I became a reasonably enthusiastic camper. I also was a Cub Scout, a Boy Scout, and at an early age, an Eagle Scout. (Decades later, I was pleased to discover that Al Shanker, long-time formidable leader of the American Federation of Teachers, had also been an

---

2. Photographs and other images appear in two sets. For an image of my grandfather, see the photo in the first set.

Eagle Scout—another tall, awkward, essentially cerebral Jew who nonetheless achieved a recognized position in a quintessentially Anglo-American institution of the day.)

To become on Eagle Scout, with the requisite twenty-one merit badges, I had to go on twenty overnight camping trips. As with camp, I initially dreaded these excursions, but eventually adapted. However, I was never converted. Those twenty long walks on dusty trails with heavy packs on my back and long nights fighting off bugs from a threadbare sleeping bag cured me forever of camping . . . to the possible regret of my children and grandchildren.

Even as I lacked the physical skills routinely acquired in team sports, scouting gave me an unusual one: I became a master driller. As part of being a Cub or Boy Scout, one is required to line up in ranks with peers and follow marching orders precisely. I may well have appeared slovenly, as I have never been known for my posture—"stand up straight," "sit straight," I can still hear my parents issuing soft directives in their slight but still recognizable German accents—but I never missed a drum beat. My skill at drilling might have been related to my musical affinity, or akin to my facility at test-taking. Whatever the reason, as with overnight camp, I am very happy that I will never again have to march and drill.

Scranton, Pennsylvania, is hardly a major media outlet. After having been a lively and expanding metropolitan area at the end of the nineteenth century, as well as a "go to" site for both vaudeville and prostitution, it had the dubious distinction of being one of the first declared "depressed areas" in the United States. When I attended movies on Saturday afternoon at the Strand Theater, I noted that Scranton was often the butt of jokes. In my naïveté, I assumed that the editors of the soundtrack had dubbed in the name of the town where the film was showing. But no! When I went to movies in college, I discovered that Scranton was still the punchline of many routines!

But however depressed and wisecrack-worthy in those days, Scranton had a few radio and television stations. When about ten years old, I joined a show called *Junior Judges* in which young people would rate various recordings, of both popular and more serious music. I did this relatively easily and well, and other Scrantonians learned to recognize my voice and my attitudes—an early taste of distinctly minor celebrityhood.

At an even younger age, I appeared on another show, this time a TV show called *Shadow Stumpers* where contestants had to recognize objects from their silhouettes. It turned out that I, the good young student in primary school, was *terrible* at doing this—so bad that, if memory serves, the host ultimately had to give me hints. I don't mind competitions and played many board games competitively with family and friends, but I resolved at that time *never* to participate in any competition that featured the recognition of visual patterns.

To the extent that young children think at all about the minds of others, we assume that *everyone* thinks and feels the way that we do. A dividend, but possible painful concomitant, of the decline of so-called childhood egocentrism, is the realization that most others have minds quite unlike our own and that our minds might even be unique in certain respects. My performance on *Shadow Stumpers* helped me to realize that I am at a distinct disadvantage when it comes to visual performances.

To begin with, I lack stereoscopic vision: I can see through only one eye at a time. Vision in my right eye is much worse than vision in my left eye; and so I will never enjoy 3D movies or indeed anything in three dimensions. Interestingly, both my maternal grandfather and my brother Erich were also essentially monocular, having a so-called lazy or wandering eye. (Erich even wore a patch over the "strong eye" in a perhaps vain effort to strengthen the other eye.) I am also quite color-blind and can hardly recognize any numbers on the Ishihara test, the standard test for color vision. To top it off, I am also prosopagnosic: I can't recognize people by their faces. This is another heritable trait, shared presumably with my father and clearly with my daughter Kerith. In fact, if I were to meet you and talk to you, I would likely say: "If I see you tomorrow, I probably won't recognize you and so I hope that you will identify yourself—and please don't take this personally." Despite the obvious superficial similarities, as far as I understand the underlying biology, these visual disorders are not related to one another.

As I grew up, I became exceedingly interested in the visual arts, even focusing on them in my doctoral dissertation and ultimately being invited to join the board of the New York Museum of Modern Art. I have developed various compensatory mechanisms, but I am distinctly handicapped initially when it comes to anything that involves vision.

What about my behavior toward others? It's not a phrase (or a characterization) that I like, but I was kind of a "goody-goody." In middle childhood, many youngsters have a strong sense of what is right and what is wrong—what psychologist Lawrence Kohlberg (reflecting the sexist nomenclature of the time) called the "good boy/bad boy" mentality. Nuance is not a primary trait of most kids, and so I easily criticized persons and actions not conforming to my own ideal of proper behavior.

In this proclivity, I was definitely helped by my parents, who were the prototypical "good Germans," always seeking to obey the letter as well as the spirit of the law.[3] I remember being read the punitive German tales of misbehaving *Max und Moritz* and *Struwwelpeter*, whose protagonists underwent a terrible denouement. Whatever authority-challenging inclinations my parents may have had as youths growing up in Weimar Germany were no doubt suppressed by life in Hitler's Germany, where a wrongly chosen word or even an inappropriate bodily movement could result in incarceration or worse. When I pass an accident of any sort, I instinctively avert my eyes and hurry on my way . . . to the astonishment of my wife and most other American peers.

Two memorable episodes from that period help to explain why I have continued to be fascinated by how we handle ethical and moral challenges, and why my work over the last twenty-five years has focused sharply on what it means to be "good."

As a child growing up in Scranton, I was a dutiful attendee of Saturday morning services at Madison Avenue Temple (also known at the time as Anshe Chesed). One Saturday morning, in the midst of a heavy snowfall, I trudged down from the hill section to attend the weekly service on the 500 block of Madison Avenue. When I arrived there, only Rabbi Erwin Herman was present—since this was a reform temple rather than an orthodox shul, all others had

---

3. You have probably heard some version of the story about the Germans who have been waiting for hours behind a sign; they foolishly fail to board the train that has issued its warning whistle and is about to depart, because they cannot bring themselves to disobey the injunction that reads "please wait behind the sign."

elected to stay home. I was all but certain that the Rabbi would cancel the service. Why bother to go through an hour or more of prayer, chanting, reading of Torah, and delivering a sermon for one dutiful preadolescent? But Rabbi Herman went through the entire service. Afterward when I asked him why he had bothered to do so for a single young congregant, he responded simply and memorably, "God does not count the house."

At around the same time, when I was in sixth grade, I had a teacher, Miss Margaret Dyer, who was the sister of John H. Dyer, the powerful superintendent of schools. At one point, Miss Dyer asked the class to recognize a tone. She then incorrectly identified it—let's say she said it was an F. I liked to get things right and so I corrected the teacher and said, probably in an all-knowing if not dismissive tone, "No, Miss Dyer, it's F sharp." Miss Dyer did not like to be challenged, and she paddled the back of my hand quite vigorously in front of the class.

I was quite upset at this public humiliation, and accordingly I reported the episode to my mother. She thought about it for a while, and then made an appointment to see the principal of the school. Hilde and I marched into Mr. Reese's office, where she recounted the episode. To my amazement, Miss Dyer was summoned into the principal's office and, despite her closeness to the very center of local power, she had to apologize to me. I have never forgotten the courage on the part of my mother (it had somehow survived life in Fascist Germany and Italy) or the sense of fair play on the part of the principal. Perhaps as a result, I try as best I can to be impartial and disinterested when I first learn of complex ethical situations, and to encourage that stance in others.

By now, you should have at least a rough idea of which skills, capacities, and abilities I have in abundance, and which ones I lack, either relatively or absolutely. If today I were meeting a clone of my preadolescent self, and had to describe him in terms of his spectrum of abilities and relative disabilities, this is what I would likely conclude using the terminology of multiple intelligences:

Language ability: very strong
Mathematical and logical abilities: strong enough
Musical abilities: quite strong
(Visual) spatial abilities: weak, probably on the basis of biological/genetic factors
Bodily kinesthetic abilities: weak, because little opportunity in childhood to practice and improve (though drilling and piano playing are possible exceptions)
Understanding of other persons: not strong
Understanding of self: average
Discriminations in the natural world (plants, animals, etc.): adequate, at least for obtaining Boy Scout merit badges
Interest in big questions: very curious about the world, especially the world of human beings, past and present

I doubt whether this kind of self-analysis would ever have occurred to me. As just noted, most ten-year-olds do not consciously compare themselves to others on a range of cognitive skills and operations. Indeed, we are inclined to think that other minds are very much like our own—and to be judgmental with respect to those with different "frames of mind." And yet, whether or not I realized it, I was a living, breathing, walking, daydreaming example of someone with a diverse spectrum of human intelligences. If I were to repeat this exercise with reference to my seventy-six -year-old persona, the profile would be quite similar—though I hope that I have somehow managed to improve my personal intelligences.

So there you have my ten-year-old self (universally called Howie at the time): a mixture of talents (reading, writing, and music) and deficits (visual and bodily); a lot of information couched somewhere in my predisciplinary psyche; considerable curiosity, especially about the human sphere of persons and politics; and a strong conscience, or what I would eventually learn to call a "powerful superego." I read a lot, listened carefully to what others were saying, and tried to make sense of it—sometimes just in my head, sometimes talking to others, usually persons older than myself, and also writing about it in thin newsletters that I continued to produce by myself and circulate sporadically throughout my childhood.

WEIGHING TESTS AND TRACKS

In 1956, the year of my bar mitzvah, my parents took me on a five-day trip to Hoboken, New Jersey, to have me "tested." My parents had a bright child on their hands and, as immigrants who had not themselves received a higher education, evidently did not quite know what to do with me. I stood out with respect both to performance on schoolwork and to my prowess on the piano (no one cared about drilling!). I hasten to add that I stood out in Scranton, Pennsylvania, then a city of no more than a hundred thousand persons, many elderly, with perhaps a thousand youngsters in my age range. There is no way of knowing whether I would have stood out in a larger and less economically depressed area. In any event, various family friends, as well as teachers and the rabbi, had suggested to my parents that we receive informed advice from trained experts. For a few hundred dollars, one could take a full battery of psychological tests at the Stevens Institute of Technology.

I have only the dimmest memory of the testing itself. It took a number of days and involved a variety of instruments. I have made several attempts to secure the actual test results or at least a list of the kinds of tests that were administered in the middle 1950s, but to no avail. I suspect that I received a full gamut of cognitive tests and, in all probability, also measures of personality, motivation, occupational skills and aspirations, and other psychological constructs of the day.[1]

But one scene is permanently etched in my memory. On the last day, we were called into the chief clinician's office, and there I heard sentences to this effect: "Mr. and Mrs. Gardner, Howard is a bright child. He can probably do most anything. But he has special gifts in the clerical area."

These words stunned me. I had been presented with literally dozens of instruments and had filled them out patiently and carefully. But apparently where I stood out, did *especially well*, was in tasks that I considered, and still consider, completely mindless. In a prototypical clerical test, the subject has to look at long strings of numbers or letters and cross out all that belong—or do not belong—to a specific category (say, cross out all of the "t"s or every other "even number"). This is a task that any trained monkey or pigeon could presumably have carried out, and today of course we would allocate such tasks to simple pattern-recognizing devices. Why had my family traveled for a week, spent hundreds of dollars (the equivalent of a few thousand dollars today), to learn something that anyone could have easily

---

1. For instance, see F. C. Thorn, *Principles of Psychological Examining: A Systematic Textbook of Applied Integrative Psychology* (Brandon, VT: Journal of Clinical Psychology, 1955).

seen and that—as far I could tell—had absolutely no bearing on future career or life choices that I might or should make? As far as I was concerned, Hoboken was hokum!

As noted, I have always been a good test-taker. But I have also become a severe critic of tests, particularly of the multiple-choice tests that were widely featured at that time. I cherish the quote attributed to the commentator William F. Buckley: "To get the right answer on one of these tests, you don't have to know what the right answer is. You just have to ferret out what the test-maker at the Educational Testing Service *thinks* is the right answer." I prefer measures that probe the capacity to think clearly, deeply, and originally. These skills don't reveal themselves in the course of hour-long short-answer tests, the kind long associated with sharpened no. 2 pencils. Even at the time, I had a definite sense that the whole week of testing did not even touch on those personal mental qualities that I now most value in others—wide reading, knowledge about many topics, the propensity to ask good questions and search for or posit reasonable answers, and at least a nascent ability to forge meaningful connections among issues—components of an emerging "synthesizing mind." In fact, in retrospect, I would go so far as to claim that the tests of the time missed all five of the "minds for the future" that I would later describe and recommend (see chapter 12).

Along with me, the chief contemporary psychological critic of intelligence and intelligence testing has been Robert J. (Bob) Sternberg. (We'll meet Bob again in later chapters.) A prolific author, Bob has written at least a dozen books and countless articles critiquing the consensus about intelligence that has long held sway within the psychometric community. While our critiques and our recommendations are quite different, we share one autobiographical feature: the inappropriate interpretation by supposedly informed others of our childhood test performances. In Bob'scase, because he did not know how to take such tests, he was classified as slow, dull, if not mentally disabled. Bob has long since disproved this misclassification! Indeed, as early as seventh grade, he created his own test of intelligence and administered it to his classmates. Bob went on to study and teach at Yale, and, thereafter, to an accomplished scholarly and administrative career in higher education.

For a young and dutiful adolescent, this testing experience was a wakeup call, a clear sign that one should not automatically accept so-called expertise. The fact that individuals may be dressed in suit and tie, have initials before or after their names, and speak with apparent authority, does not guarantee that they know what they are talking about. Of course, I wanted eventually to acquire expertise myself—in what field, I did not yet know—but I was already inclined to challenge what I was told, whether by my sixth-grade teacher or the psychologists in Hoboken.

So, having an offspring who (at his bar mitzvah) had been declared a "man" and (at his testing) a future clerk (!), the Gardner family was faced with two decisions. The first and easier one concerned my piano playing. My parents had not even planned to give me music lessons. But as I've mentioned, when I was six years old, we visited a friend's home and I had begun to pick out pieces on their piano, just playing by ear. This ability was sufficiently unusual that the friends recommended that my parents purchase a piano. Impoverished though our family was in 1950, my parents bought a Sohmer upright for $30, which remained a fixture in our living room through my high school years.

I was fortunate in my teachers. Geri Friedlin (later Berg) was a tall woman who wore long dark skirts and dresses that reached to her ankles. She was a friend of the family—upon his arrival in Scranton in late 1938, my father had ported gasoline tanks for her uncle Ike. Geri herself had commuted to New York City to take lessons with master teacher Alfred Mirovitch. I took weekly lessons with her, and practiced daily, often with my mother, who as a girl had also studied piano, by my side. I advanced quickly through the Schirmer primers and began to play easy pieces such as Hanon and Czerny exercises, and short Bach and Mozart compositions. Geri was the perfect first teacher; by words and by example, she introduced me to the romance of music making. After a few years, Geri said that she had taught me what she could. She suggested that I go to study with Harold Briggs, who worked with more advanced students.

I wish photographs or news stories about Harold Briggs were available. He was quite a character. Easily in his nineties when I began to study with him in the early 1950s, he lived alone in a second-floor studio apartment with two grand pianos that he treated like members of his family. Amazingly energetic, he would bound up the stairs to his flat. He had a small cohort of students who performed for one another every month or so—a time-tested way of monitoring one's own progress and comparing oneself with one's peers. With Mr. Briggs, I took on more challenging pieces like the Mozart and Beethoven sonatas that are now part of the so-called standard repertoire. Clearly, I was one of his star students, and probably one of the best young students in Scranton (which, as I've noted, was a small pond). Around the time of my testing in Hoboken, Mr. Briggs said to me, "Now you have to get serious. You need to practice at least two to three hours a day, and you should probably work with a teacher in New York."

For me, the decision was surprisingly easy. I liked playing the piano for others—family, friends, fellow students—and, importantly, for myself. But I had no wish to practice several hours a day nor to commute to New York (at that time, four to five hours each way, by bus or train). And so I declared, "I guess I'll stop formal lessons." And so I did. After a while, I resumed playing with my first teacher, Geri Berg, but this time we played together pieces for four hands, arrangements that were as new to her as they were to me.

In retrospect, my decision to give up formal instruction in music reveals a kind of iconoclasm that has long characterized my relation to formal study. I was perfectly happy to continue playing on *my* terms, but I was reluctant, if not unwilling, to follow the tried-and-true path of further formal study in the acknowledged discipline in the prescribed manner. I have a strong superego, but one that reflects my own predilections. I was not going to be a pianist, but I did not stop making music. Through high school and college and into graduate school, I played—and even practiced—when I could, improvised at school parties, and gave piano lessons to a few individuals as a means of making extra money. Nowadays, whenever I am not traveling, I play scales and favorite pieces from the repertoire for at least a half-hour every day. Most important, a critical part of my research and scholarship has been in the psychology of the arts, with music always central in my mind.

At some level, I had already sensed in my teens that artistic competence was not the same as being competent in academic schoolwork. So to speak, IQ is not the same as AQ. As students in possession of a singular talent advance in school in the United

States, a significant dividing line emerges. Suppose a student is much better in an area of talent—piano playing, chess, cartooning, dance, or a sport—than in his or her schoolwork. There will be pressure to continue lessons in that area and to become skillful enough so that this talent, as it were, becomes one's meal ticket to future options, including admission to a selective college or conservatory and, if fortunate, career success.

If, however, the talented student is also good at schoolwork, there is much less pressure to continue in the talent area; and in almost all cases, there is far more reward for excelling in the standard curricula and tests of school. I was the proverbial good student. So long as I remained successful in scholastic matters, whether I pursued piano (and whether a peer chose to pursue tennis or theater, chess or cheerleading) was completely up to me. While my artistic focus in childhood was chiefly music, I did travel frequently to New York to attend Broadway shows, first with my mother, later with a school friend, Ron Gordon, who eventually became a graphic artist. As a high school student, I also traveled with family or friends to western Massachusetts to attend summer concerts given at Tanglewood by the Boston Symphony Orchestra. I even frequented the local museum in Scranton. For me, the arts have always complemented standard academic subjects.

The second major decision my parents and I faced in my early teens was where I should go to secondary school. We suspected that nearby Scranton Central High School would be unlikely to stretch me, but it was by far the most convenient alternative. And so with my classmates from James Madison and John Audubon K–8 elementary schools, I began to matriculate at the high school, located at the edge of the town center. I took the requisite college prep curriculum, while continuing relatively undemanding involve-ments with the Youth Group at my temple and my Boy Scout troop.

But soon enough, something became clear to me. Not only was high school not challenging, but, and here I choose my words care-fully, in some subjects I even knew more than the teachers (shades of my contretemps in sixth grade with Miss Dyer). And so I began to consider switching schools.

Again, relying on the advice of people more informed about options, my parents pushed me to attend Phillips Academy in Andover, Massachusetts. Then as now, Andover (as it is usually called) was a first-rate secondary school, which in that day placed its graduates largely in Ivy League colleges. But I was adamant: I did not want to leave home entirely and live with individuals I did not know, and whose backgrounds were likely to be far more privileged than mine.

We compromised on a local independent school, Wyoming Sem-inary, in nearby Kingston, Pennsylvania, where I could live during the week but easily come home on the weekends. Clearly, Wyo-ming Seminary was not Andover. No one would confuse the two in terms of curriculum or student body or the success achieved by alumni. But "Sem" represented a shrewd middle ground between the familiar and unchallenging environment of Scranton Central High School and the greater intellectual and social demands of an elite preparatory school far from home. This choice also gave me the opportunity, at least for a few more years, to be one of the bigger fish in a middle-sized pond.

More than thirty years ago, I attended my twenty-fifth high school reunion at Wyoming Seminary. Before the trip I had minimized the importance of high school, placing a far greater emphasis on my several decades as a student, researcher, and faculty member at Harvard University. But a few hours back on the high school campus, like Proust's madeleine, awakened copious memories, and I came to realize that high school had in many ways been transformative for me.

Growing up in Scranton, I had been largely surrounded by family and neighbors. In high school I began encountering students from many different communities and a variety of backgrounds. I had previously paid little or no attention to my clothing, my grooming, my overall appearance; now I began to notice what others were wearing and how they presented themselves. I discovered girls and began to date.

If you look at my high school yearbook, you might conclude— quite rightly—that I was one of the most involved persons on campus, a member of many organizations and a leader of a few. You might even conclude—wrongly—that I was a "big man on campus." At most, I was one of several bigger men and women. Certainly, I did not think of myself at the time as standing out; I was far too conscious of my marginal status, as a nonwealthy, five-day-a-week boarder with parents who had not gone to college and who spoke English with an accent. But at that high school reunion I learned, to my complete surprise, that I had occupied an outsized role in the psyche of others who apparently felt threatened by my accomplishments. That saddened me.

In my three years at Wyoming Seminary, I had two experiences that, in retrospect, could be termed transformative. Shortly after arriving, I tried out for the school publication the *Opinator*. (In addition to the various newspapers that I had produced in elementary school, I had also joined the newspaper at Scranton Central High

School.) Both the name and the publication were unusual, perhaps unique in secondary schools of the era: the *Opinator* appeared weekly, and contained news, sports, editorials, poetry, and fiction as well as advertisements and block prints. It had an illustrated cover, and in that sense as well, looked more like the *New Yorker* than the *New York Times*. It was edited entirely by students, who also raised money through the securing of advertisements, and several of us involved in the newspaper spent at least as much time with it as with our studies.

On the *Opinator*, I began as a reporter but soon moved to the editorial desk. With a friend, Barry Yoselson, I became future coeditor in my junior year and coeditor in my senior year. Clearly, I was learning about journalism and how to run a small organization; I worked with and supervised (and occasionally fired) fellow students; but I was also trying out my own ideas and honing my own literary, editing, and marketing skills. In looking through now-yellowed pages of several dozen issues, I have been amazed to discover what caught my adolescent interest.[2] I had written about many of the topics that I studied decades later. Among my journalistic output were articles about liberal arts, test taking, college admission, and even a review of James Conant's 1959 book, *The American High School*.

The other transformative experience occurred in a so-called senior seminar, taught by historian John Betterly and literary scholar Frank Light. The senior seminar was restricted to a small group of strong students and focused on US history and literature. The course was distinguished by its reading list: we read many classical American

---

2. As I detail in my blog, https://howardgardner.com/2018/05/31/the
-child-as-father-to-the-man/.

novels (*Adventures of Huckleberry Finn*, *The Scarlet Letter*, *Moby-Dick*, *An American Tragedy*, *The Great Gatsby*, *The Grapes of Wrath*) and also learned about the literary figures of the time, whether or not we read their work. Of more significance to me, instead of learning from a single textbook, we read works of historical analysis. I carefully read, reread, and underlined Richard Hofstadter's *The American Political Tradition*, Eric Goldman's *The Age of Reform*, Vernon Parrington's *Main Currents of American Thought*, and a memorably formidable monograph, *The American Revolution Considered as a Social Movement*, by J. Franklin Jameson. Each week we had to write a paper on history, literature, or their synthesis.

Clearly, by both syllabus and design, this was a college-type course, designed specifically as preparation for attendance at an American liberal arts college. Notably, the works I treasured were not standard historical narratives ("first A happened, then B") but rather works of synthesis. In particular, I admired Hofstadter's versatility. He could take a complex topic like the careers of notable American presidents and delineate the intellectual and political currents that led to their election and then guided or undermined their tenure in office and their ultimate legacies. Hofstadter wrote about figures and events—Lincoln, the two Roosevelts, the Civil War—in ways that transcended the two-dimensional treatments I had previously encountered in the conventional Landmark book or high school textbook. For the first time in my life, I came to realize that historical figures were not cinematic heroes or villains but human beings who had complex motivations, who were faced with choices, who could have acted in different ways with different outcomes. And for the first time, I realized that authors (like Hofstadter) had "voices" themselves—putting forth their own viewpoints and arguing, sometimes explicitly, with their own teachers as well as with acknowledged experts in their disciplines.

I thoroughly enjoyed the course, did well in it, and seemed geared to major in history in college. Only later, as I'll describe early in the next chapter, did I discover the limits of the course—or more precisely, the limits of my engagement in the course.

Other than my teachers and the individuals encountered in my reading, two other persons, quite different from one another, exerted powerful and enduring influences on me during my teen years. One was my uncle, Fred (Fritz) Gardner. Like others in my parents' generation whose life choices were undermined by the rise of Hitler, Fritz had never attended college. But Fritz was both a genuine polymath and a genuine intellectual. This autodidact had become an expert on eighteenth-century British literary history, and had assembled an increasingly valuable collection of first edition children's books.[3] He flew his own plane, built (or at least rebuilt) his own computer, played chess with considerable skill, loved dogs, and over the years had girlfriends in several locations. Without children himself, and in an obviously unsatisfying marriage, Fritz took me under his wing, talked with me about all sorts of topics, gave me myriads of advice (much of which I remember to this day, not all of which I followed), introduced me to books and art, took me on trips with him on his plane, and even took the time to send me written critiques of my articles in the *Opinator*. Finally, though I have only come to realize this recently, Fritz was a natural and gifted synthesizer—interested in everything, eager to make sense

3. Today one can visit the Frederick Gardner collection at the Free Library of Philadelphia.

and connections, but not unduly burdened by the constraints and strictures of a particular academic discipline.

Something that Fritz did with a light touch ultimately had a life-long influence on me. When I was a teenager, he gave me a psychology textbook. I think that he sensed, before I did, that I had a lot of interest in the topics of psychology, even though I was not at the time aware of the discipline per se. Thanks to my experience at the Stevens Institute, I did know about psychological tests, but did not realize that there was a much broader study of how the human mind works. I remember leafing through Norman Munn's textbook many times, and being especially intrigued by the tests for color-blindness. I knew, of course, that I was color-blind and that this was a sex-linked hereditary condition; but I had not realized that there were varieties of color-blindness, and I was fascinated by the theories of how color vision worked, and the rationale behind the hitherto mysterious Ishihara test. Though neither of us could have anticipated it at the time, Fritz had planted in me the seed for studying psychology and perhaps pursuing it as a career . . . and perhaps even for one day writing textbooks on that subject!

The other individual, Mark Harris, was more of a peer, just two years older. Mark came from the other side of Scranton, literally and figuratively. In the late 1920s his mother had gone to Welles-ley College, and his father—a leading lawyer in northeastern Pennsylvania—had gone to Harvard College. Somewhat to my surprise, I had been invited to Mark's bar mitzvah, and in preparation for the customary postceremony party, had taken my first dance lessons. (These proved worthless in light of my meager bodily kin-esthetic intelligence.)

Though he could presumably have gone to any secondary school, Mark had chosen to attend Wyoming Seminary (or his family had made that choice for him). Mark became a role model and, to my benefit, a friend. I pursued many of the same activities that he had pursued. He had been editor of the *Opinator* and I followed in his footsteps. When I had roommate problems, he generously allowed me to bunk with him until I could find a single room in the dormitory. We shared some friends, girls as well as boys. Mark was self-directed, a trait that I admired and have sought to emulate. And most important, Mark was admitted to and attended Harvard College, matriculating and then graduating two years before me. Without Mark's example, I might well have chosen another educational path, which could have led to another life story altogether.

Clearly, I was fortunate to have these two mentors and role models. Only in retrospect do I realize that they probably saw some appealing features in me as well; mentors and mentees experience mutual connections. And because I had the good luck of being a white male born near the middle of the twentieth century, good potential mentors have been available to me throughout my life.

Ah, college. Even in those less intensely competitive days, attending college was on the minds of upwardly mobile students from northeastern Pennsylvania. As early as my sophomore year in high school, I took the PSAT, and thereafter, a bundle of College Board achievement and aptitude tests, doing well on them. In the summers after my sophomore and junior years, my father took me on tours of several colleges in the northeast (almost no one flew in those days, so college visits had to be within driving distance). When even younger, I had read a classic comic book and, on its historically oriented back cover, learned about three marshals of a class at Harvard—one Catholic, one Protestant, one Jewish. As someone always conscious of my ethnic background, this apparent latitudinarianism made a favorable impression on me. And so, in my heart (if not said aloud), I dreamt of going to Harvard College.

I've already made a few allusions to the fact that I am not very conscious of my appearance; being color-blind and otherwise limited in visual acuity does not help. During my college-looking trip to Harvard, I dressed as best I could. Many years later, a friend of mine who worked at the college snuck a look at my admissions dossier, where she discovered that the interviewer had noted that I was wearing a red tie and red socks—noticeable, I suppose, in those days (and perhaps today as well).

I remembered the name of the interviewer, Peter Frost, and that he had appeared to be very "preppy." A few years ago, I saw a letter in the newspaper from a Williams College professor named Peter Frost. I decided to write to him and find out whether he had in fact been my interviewer. Turns out that Peter—now an emeritus professor of history—had indeed been an interviewer for Harvard College back in the day. And, since it is unlikely that there had been two interviewers with that name, he had in fact interviewed me and placed that "red" note in my dossier.

Peter and I got together and had a good laugh about this incident and the concomitant coincidence. He said that he had stopped interviewing prospective students when he had learned that admissions was interested chiefly in recruiting athletes and in avoiding too many pre-med students from New Jersey. I sometimes wonder whether things have gotten any better since I applied to college sixty years ago.

DISCOVERING ENDURING INTERESTS AND
ALLURING APPROACHES

One remembers far more from one's freshman year in college than from any of the remaining three years—at least, that's what I'd bet on. Psychologists call it a *primacy effect*. And we contrast that with a *recency effect*: our often less vivid memories of breakfast yesterday morning, a conversation last evening, the full name of a new acquaintance or of a new personage in the news.

That primacy effect has certainly operated in my case. Especially if fueled by an old photo or by reference to an incident from that John F. Kennedy/Camelot era, I could talk at great length about Harvard College in 1961—boring everyone except me and, possibly, a few classmates in the process.

Two quite vivid memories from the beginning of my freshmen year frame my experience as what we might today term a "first-gen" student in Harvard College.

The first episode took place before classes had even officially begun. A reception for incoming students was held in capacious Harvard yard. I struck up a conversation with a new classmate, David Gould.[1] The two of us walked up the steps of the imposing Widener Library. Having traversed the several dozen steps, we beheld the large space dotted by hundreds of classmates and a few administrators and teachers, and agreed: "The world is now open to us; there are no limits to what we can achieve."

Of course, that was a dual-edged aspiration, because if we could succeed big, we could also fail big (and both of us skirted that edge in the years ahead). But for both of us, first-generation college students from humble backgrounds, and not having attended elite prep schools, the prospect of four years in Cambridge, Massachusetts— where we were free to study whatever we wanted to study, hang out where we liked with those whom we liked, and pursue any of a myriad of other interests—was overwhelming, but also inflected distinctly in a positive direction.

As a fledgling student of American history, I could not avoid being struck, and more than a little intimidated, by the storied grounds to which we had been admitted, and upon which we now gazed and on which we also trod. In front of us was Emerson Hall, named after arguably the first intellectual giant of United States, philosopher Ralph Waldo Emerson. And within easy distance (and quick recall) were traces of Emerson's essayist friend Henry David Thoreau, William James (America's most illustrious philosopher),

---

1. David became a treasured friend. Tragically, he was killed in the explosion in December 1988 of Pan Am flight 103, over Lockerbie, Scotland.

Walter Lippmann (the leading political commentator of "our" time). And going beyond the ranks of white men (who still dominated the college), we were aware as well of W. E. B. Du Bois, the leading black intellectual of the era, Ralph J. Bunche (a distinguished diplomat as well the first black overseer at Harvard), and Helen Keller, the deaf and blind woman who attended Radcliffe College (soon to be merged with Harvard College) and went on to a brilliant life in letters and service. We aspired to seek our place within the ranks of these luminaries—several of whom I had been introduced to in that pivotal senior seminar at "Wyo Sem."

The second memorable episode was a little more humbling. Whatever extracurricular sirens, sites, and schoolmates beckoned, I had to select courses as well. That proved to be relatively easy, at least in my freshman year. I took a survey course in world history, a survey course in music, the introductory course in biology, the introductory course in economics, a required writing course, and a freshman seminar. The latter course was a recent addition to the Harvard curriculum. Funded by a then-anonymous gift from the inventor of instant photography, Edwin Land of Polaroid Land camera fame, these seminars gave small groups of students the opportunity to work directly with scholars on research topics.

In view of my well-established interest in history, I selected a seminar on "topics in American history" given by Stanley (Stan) Katz. The course, with fewer than ten students, focused on original documents from two famous historical cases, both occurring in Massachusetts. The first was the Salem witch trials of the 1690s, in which hapless young women were accused, tried, and sometimes hanged. The second case was the Sacco and Vanzetti affair of the

1920s, where two immigrants with anarchistic tendencies had been convicted of murder and put to death.[2]

A first seminar paper on some facet of the witch trials was assigned, and I confidently wrote my five pages. I say "confidently" because I had done the reading carefully and I was a certified good writer—after all, I had edited the *Opinator* at high school and had been placed in an advanced honors section of the writing course required for all freshmen at Harvard.

Imagine my shock when I received the paper back with generous scribblings by Dr. Katz throughout and, most damagingly, the final note, "Isn't this a first draft?"

Stan Katz's comment was a wake-up call. To borrow a phrase from Immanuel Kant, the great eighteenth-century philosopher, I had been abruptly awakened from my dogmatic slumbers. Until this point in my young academic life, I had thought that my job was to do the reading, think about it, and then write a careful summary, perhaps suggesting an idea or two along the way. "Give it back clearly and accurately" might have been my rule of thumb.

But thinking about it and having subsequent talks with Stan Katz, as well as with other students, I realized that I now needed to embark on a far more ambitious, arduous, and risky mission. Of course, digest and reflect; but then put forth trenchant criticisms,

---

2. Both cases had Harvard links: Puritan minister and author Cotton Mather, whose father had been president of Harvard, was the presiding judge at one of the Salem trials; a special tribunal created to decide the fate of Sacco and Vanzetti had been presided over by Abbott Lawrence Lowell, at the time the president of Harvard; and Lowell, who favored execution, was publicly opposed by Felix Frankfurter, then a major professor at Harvard Law School and later Associate Justice of the United States Supreme Court.

raise intriguing questions, perhaps even propose a new way of thinking about the issues. To use a phrase that we have recently coined in our own work on higher education, I was expected to display "liberal arts capital"—in this case, poring over historical documents and trying to make sense of them in light of all of our knowledge and insights. And, to borrow from my understanding of historian Richard Hofstadter's achievement, I was now expected to exhibit my own "voice."

Let me characterize this experience, retroactively, in terms of the themes of this book. Ever since I had begun to write book reviews and class papers, I had seen my job as synthesizing what I had known and what I had read. I did not simply parrot back or paraphrase what I had learned; mere *summarization* was not enough in high school, let alone in college. But it did not occur to me that I should simply use that synthesized knowledge as background and as a springboard: casting the embedded themes, ideas, concepts in a new way, or, even better, coming up with a wholly new or at least a fresh way of characterizing the issues.

These days I conceptualize this point in terms of a *continuum of synthesis*. At one end is the *conventional synthesis*: just bringing concepts and ideas together in a way that relies heavily on common sense or conventional wisdom and would unlikely be disputed in any way. That is what I had largely done throughout my schooling— and what I still look for in a reasonably edited textbook or search engine.

Now I was expected to create an *original synthesis*: an account that demonstrated that I had read and mastered the existing material (usually texts, but this could also include works of art) but went beyond the task of weaving sources together and instead put forth new ideas, contrasts, and questions. So this is what college was really about![3]

Of course, this epiphany, like other damascene experiences, is easier to describe in retrospect. I suspect that at the time, I was just peeved and uncertain. I wish that I had documentary evidence of my succeeding papers, as I have evidence of my thinking and jottings during my editorial stint at the *Opinator* and my notes and drafts once I had finished my doctoral studies.

Alas, that access is impossible. Like most pack rats, I saved all of my papers from school, storing them in the garage at our family's home in Scranton. Once or twice my father asked me what I was going to do with this literary output, and I imagine that I just shrugged his questions off. Then one vacation, when I returned home to Scranton, I noticed that the several dozen boxes of juvenilia were no longer in the garage. When I asked where they were now stored, I received the unwelcome news that my father had simply thrown them away. Pressed, he said "Well, I thought you did not want them, and I needed the space for something else."

In the opening chapter of this book, I said that I gave my parents an A. This unexpected loss angered me, but if it's the worst criticism I can make of my father, I have no reason to change the high grade. I also realize that I share some of the responsibility since I did not make clear to Dad *why* my school papers were worth saving—if indeed they were. It does mean that this memoir draws less on documents

---

3. I would now add that a college freshman is unlikely to say anything *wholly* original about two heavily studied cases—but at the least the student must carry out an analysis that goes beyond the routine in content or form, and preferably beyond both.

from my higher education that I would have wished. And my father's "bonfire of my vanities" spares future biographers—in the unlikely event there are any—the need to read old sloppily typed papers, get their hands dirty from handling ancient carbon paper, and squint to decipher fading comments offered by attentive, dutiful or critical instructors. Fortunately, the *Opinator* issues and those four papers from the senior seminar still remain, but they are relatively slim pickings in light of the scores of other papers—including various fledgling syntheses—that I wrote in four years of high school, four years of college, and five years of graduate school.

In the absence of appreciable documentary evidence, one relies perforce on other artifacts. I did well in my freshman year at Harvard College and received a Detur Prize: my choice of any book, on which the Harvard seal would be prominently embossed. In retrospect my choice is both surprising (if not bizarre) and revealing. I chose *A Literary History of the United States*, an extended and expensive encyclopedic work assembled by four eminent literary scholars, which covers, in a few pages each, nearly all significant American writers up until the middle of the twentieth century.

I suspect that I made this selection because, as a graduate of the senior seminar at Wyoming Seminary, and in view of my then scholarly aspirations at Harvard, it would be useful to have a source book—indeed, a work of synthesis—that would have been costly to purchase and that I could place near my desk for easy and frequent reference (just as I kept an encyclopedia alongside my bed when I was a kid, and as I keep the *Oxford English Dictionary* next to my writing desk until this day). Perhaps I was hoping to nurture my internal Edmund Wilson, who was becoming a literary hero at the time. Perhaps I thought that the selection would also be seen by others as a "scholarly" one. Today I shudder at the selection because it seems so impersonal and bureaucratic and unimaginative. Why not Proust in French, or the drawings of Michelangelo, or the collected writings of Sir Isaac Newton, spanning mathematics to alchemy? But the selection also reveals how I thought about things: I wanted works full of information about my interests; I did not care how my choice looked to others.

Some words about Edmund Wilson. Born in 1895, educated at the Hill (Preparatory) School and at Princeton, Wilson became America's best-known man of letters, to use a phrase of the day. Fundamentally a journalist (he had no advanced degree and never held a significant teaching position or indeed any other job except occasional editor), Wilson wrote clearly and insightfully on an amazing number of topics ranging from the rise of symbolism in literature to the founding of the Soviet Union to the quality of translations of Russian classics. He published at least thirty books and no doubt a thousand articles. I became interested in whatever Wilson wrote about, just because he was such a good writer. (Come to think of it, that's an apt definition of what it means to be a good writer!) Wilson could introduce a reader to an area about which the reader knew nothing—symbolist writing in French and in English, in *Axel's Castle*, for example—and make one feel able to hold an intelligent conversation about it. He could also take a topic about which one thought one was knowledgeable, and surprise the reader with new information—as he did in *To the Finland Station*, pinpointing the origins of the Soviet Union in French scholarly writing in the early nineteenth century.

I myself was beginning to aspire to become a writer who could cover many topics, and do so in a way that was accessible to the intelligent layperson. Though I did not realize it at the time, that aspiration would find itself in perennial tension with the disciplinary training that I was to receive after college. For now, to return to an earlier analogy, the facts and information were beginning to group within certain lanes—the historical lane, the biographical lane, the literary lane—but the disciplinary borders were still porous, and I was by temperament inclined to keep them that way. Rather than putting a stake centrally within history, I wanted to be free to draw on other perspectives.

As a result of my credible freshman record, I had the opportunity to compete for another honor, the Jacob Wendell Prize. In this particular case, I had to be interviewed by a committee. As with my interview at Harvard some years before, I dressed as best I could, perhaps avoiding the embarrassingly tell-tale red tie and red socks that Peter Frost had unknowingly chronicled for posterity. I have no memory of the interview per se, but I do remember meeting the individual who won the prize. As soon as I met my classmate David Gordon, I realized why he had been selected (and why I had not). Unlike my friend David Gould, this particular David came from an academic background, with no fewer than three eminent economists in his family; he had gone to an elite secondary school; and he already seemed poised for a subsequent interview for the Rhodes scholarship. I instantly concluded that however good I was able to look on paper, I did not know how to conduct myself in a high-stakes interview for a prestigious prize at Harvard College (or indeed anywhere else). Synthesizing on paper—Wyoming Seminary or Harvard College style—was an entirely different enterprise than synthesizing orally while on your feet in a high-stress situation. I realized that in addition to being able to write well, I would have to learn to speak effectively in different settings.

A chronic believer in self-improvement—in possession of what is nowadays labeled a "growth mindset"—I decided immediately to take a course on speaking and rhetoric. I wanted to acquire the "voice of authority" that I had not needed before but that would presumably serve me well as I pursued my professional ambitions (not that I had a clue yet about what they were!). When I showed up for the course, I discovered a student cohort I hadn't expected: those for whom English was not a first language, and who wanted to learn to speak English well. The course was decidedly *not* for someone who had simply failed to garner a significant prize. I did not remain enrolled in the course; but I became a friend of the instructor, Ellsworth Fersch, a Cambridge character who would be well worth a book, but not, alas, this one.

Another Proustian memory. Recently at a family celebration, my grandson Oscar, then age thirteen, gave a toast. All of a sudden, I remembered what happened to me at age thirteen. My father gave me a book about public speaking and inscribed it: "All my life I have regretted my inability to give a good speech. I hope that this book will help you to speak well."

How to summarize, or perhaps more aptly, how to synthesize, four intense years of study and innumerable conversations with peers as well as teachers?

My interests shifted. As a freshman, in my history course, I had been impressed by the recently published prize-winning book *Young Man Luther*. This biography of the founder of Protestantism, by psychoanalyst Erik Erikson, represented a pioneering effort at *psychohistory*: an ambitious and daring scholarly attempt to explain key ideas, concepts, and media of communication associated with Martin Luther in light of his personal psychological development.[4] My history instructor, Ron Witt, noted my interest in Erikson's work. He suggested that I learn more about psychoanalysis and psychology—terms known to me because Uncle Fritz had given me a copy of Norman Munn's textbook, with its revealing illustrations and explanation of the condition of color-blindness.

Nonetheless, history was a subject familiar to me, and I liked it. So I dutifully decided to major—"concentrate" is the Harvard lingo—in history. I enrolled in the sophomore tutorial, a small seminar in which concentrators read and discuss the study of history. A replay, I hoped, of the freshman seminar with Stan Katz. Unfortunately, I did not resonate with the readings, and the tutor was no Stan Katz. The readings were neither history nor psychohistory, but rather historiography: essays by famous historians on how they go about researching and writing history.

With the benefit of hindsight, I understand why these works were assigned, and years later, given my interests in methodologies of the scholarly disciplines, I might have enjoyed or at least profited from reading them. But at the time I found them precious, obtuse, abstruse, and "inside baseball," written for people older and more reflective and more "metacognitive" than I was at the time. It also means I might not have liked graduate school in history any more than I liked graduate school in psychology—a tale told in the next chapter.

And so, to import another psychological term, I fell prey to an "avoidance." I no longer looked forward to my tutorial. On the

---

4. Believe it or not, Erikson makes much of Luther's episodes and struggles on the toilet!

other hand, I was thoroughly enjoying my second history course, Oscar Handlin's survey of American social history—a field that the Brooklyn-born intellectual polymath had virtually invented—and I had liked the Eriksonian and psychohistorical adventures of the previous year. And so I looked into a field called "Social Relations," a relatively new concentration and one, to be frank, that was often chosen by athletes (we called them "jocks") because it was seen as relatively easy (a "gut") compared, say, to physics, linguistics, or other ostensibly more demanding disciplines.

The more I learned about "Soc Rel" (as this neologism was universally abbreviated—pronounced "sock rell"), the more I thought that I would enjoy it. Certainly no one would take me, with my modest bodily kinesthetic talents, for a "jock." And so, I switched concentrations, took two introductory Soc Rel courses, and enrolled in a tutorial in Soc Rel, in which we read fundamental social science sources—Karl Marx on communism, Max Weber on capitalism, Emile Durkheim on the organization of societies—ones that were chock full of exciting ideas and (unlike the tutorial in history) not primarily methodological or metadisciplinary.

In this particular major, I was a star (whether that would have been the case in other majors, including history, remains unclear). I have two pieces of evidence for this self-congratulatory characterization. First, at the end of my sophomore year, the head of the undergraduate program, George Goethals, told me that I was free to design my own course of study for the next two years. I very much doubt that this option was offered to students in other departments, no matter how strong the students were. The second piece of evidence came when Erik Erikson, author of the study of Luther and recently appointed professor at Harvard, was scheduled to offer a junior tutorial. Because he was brilliant, handsome, charismatic, intellectually accessible, and promised to give us insights into our own "identity crises," dozens of students applied for admission.

Goethals was a fair-minded person but not one who was blind to optics (as we might now phrase it). He announced that he would select the students by lot, but as soon as I entered the seminar room and saw the eleven other students, it was clear to me that the members of the Erikson seminar had been handpicked, probably by Goethals himself. Indeed, they would have been excellent students in other majors, not just in Soc Rel. We were pretty big fish, even at Harvard College. Clearly, the head tutor of the program wanted Erikson to be impressed by Harvard students and so left nothing to chance.

What *was* the field of Social Relations? This poorly named concentration reminds me of an academic camel—an academic department created by a committee of scholarly stars. In this case, immediately after World War II (in 1946), several then prominent Harvard researchers in the social sciences joined forces to create a new department. The chief luminaries and architects of this deliberately multidisciplinary department were Talcott Parsons in sociology, Gordon Allport in psychology, and Clyde Kluckhohn in anthropology; and the research and teaching that they envisioned consisted of an amalgam of those three disciplines.

Despite the ill-chosen name and the chameleon origin, the Soc Rel idea and scholarly program was a good and important one. The lines between anthropology (the study of humans, from prehistory and across cultures, especially preliterate ones in remote corners of the globe), sociology (the study of groups, organizations, and societies), and psychology (the study of individual behavior, personality, motivation, and cognition) are very thin. Efforts to separate and compartmentalize them are artificial and unconvincing.

In retrospect, I can see that this department was made-to-order for individuals with a synthesizing mind, especially individuals interested in what one might call, if somewhat pretentiously, the human condition or human nature. For one thing, it deliberately combined a number of academic disciplines—psychology, sociology, anthropology, shards of political science and economics—and invited practitioners to draw on insights and concepts from these several perspectives. For another, while it certainly drew on the current methods of statistics and experiments in the laboratory, Soc Rel gave plenty of room to those of us who were more drawn to thematic analyses and to portraits of major phenomena than to cumulative studies of single and deliberately simplified phenomena (for example, kinship structures in preliterate societies, a favorite of anthropologists, or the memorization of nonsense syllables, a staple of psychologists). It was as much a department of books and of book writers as it was a department of scholarly papers and multiple empirical studies of a single phenomenon. And it was also a department whose members often wrote for the intelligent general reader, though none wrote as elegantly as Edmund Wilson and few wrote as powerfully as Richard Hofstadter, my authorial heroes of the time (and thereafter). Soc Rel scholars were not scientists with large laboratories equipped with fancy equipment, but they were also not literary scholars, let alone artists. They believed that they were launching a new science or a new set of interlocking sciences.

But two other, less grand motivations also underwrote the department. One was opportunistic: American foundations, and, increasingly, the federal government, were very interested in the possibility of a *science* of human nature. Events and creations in the recent World War such as propaganda, brainwashing, and communication theory were very much on their minds, and not far from their checkbooks. The leaders of Soc Rel discerned the chance to accumulate significant funding. Indeed, as poignantly described by Robert Nisbet, himself a sociologist, in his book *The Degradation of the Academic Dogma*, the opportunity for large-scale funding brought about a fundamental change in power and responsibilities in universities—a situation about which many, including me, still have highly ambivalent feelings. Are we, as educators of the carefully chosen young people, there primarily to teach and nurture students, with the professor on one end of a log, and the student on the other? Or is our primary task to carry out research and publication in scholarly venues? Or is it some awkward amalgam of these two activities, ones handled quite separately in many other countries? I've wrestled with this tension for decades.

The other motivation for the founding (and the funding!) of Soc Rel was reactionary or antagonistic. Each of the constituent disciplines contained a division between those who were hard-nosed and quantitative—whom William James had dubbed the "tough minded"—and those who were qualitative, interpretive, far less committed to mathematical models and explanations—whom James had called "the tender minded." Those attracted to Soc Rel wanted to distinguish themselves from mathematical sociologists, behaviorist psychologists, and physical anthropologists, and for a while they did so quite successfully. Soc Rel was to some extent a refuge for those who were interested in big questions and were not afraid to deal with messy phenomena, albeit imperfectly. Its fate could be analyzed retrospectively in terms of the key disciplines: future anthropologists would look at the tribal nature of academics, future sociologists at the organization of disciplines in the academy, future psychologists at the personal motivations of succeeding generations of academic "stars." And those educated in Soc Rel might have sought to synthesize this trio of analyses.

In 1972, a quarter of a century after Soc Rel was founded, the leadership of the university decided to close it down. Similar decisions were being made at other so-called peer institutions that had hitherto encouraged, or at least tolerated, interdisciplinary work in the human sciences. Such decisions are not made lightly, especially when large egos are involved. In this particular case, the founders had all retired, as had the initial funders; the pioneers had failed to groom sufficiently worthy or powerful successors; and the promise of an integrated new social science had not been fulfilled. In fact, in a sharp but fundamentally accurate postmortem, Charles Dollard, then president of the Carnegie Corporation, a major funder, declared: "A great deal of time is wasted on premature attempts to produce very large 'syntheses' or 'integrations' of social science fields."[5]

There were also intrinsic reasons for the fading of Soc Rel. Each of the constituent disciplinarians had strong loyalty to the fields in which he (or occasionally she) was trained; and so ultimately Harvard and other schools, like Yale and Chicago, reverted to the *status quo ante bellum*: separate departments of psychology, sociology, and anthropology. As could have been predicted as well, each reborn department now contained within it, indeed recreated, the strains

---

5. Quoted in Roger Geiger, *American Higher Education after World War II* (Princeton, NJ: Princeton University Press, 2019), 99.

that had led in the first place to the formation of an amalgamated department in the aftermath of America's triumphant military victories. Within each of the reborn disciplinary departments, one could readily locate those who leaned toward methodological impeccability in pursuing tractable issues, and those who in contrast aimed to illuminate far bigger and messier issues, using whatever methods could be entrained in whatever way seemed defensible.

Why this potted academic history? To this day, I remain a staunch believer in the mission of the Department of Social Relations. So did a large number of individuals who were trained in the heyday of Soc Rel, though we are now distinctly senior—Rick Shweder, Claude Fischer, William Damon from Harvard, Mihaly Csikszentmihalyi, trained at University of Chicago—or alas, now deceased—Robert Bellah, Clifford Geertz, and Neil Smelser, just to name a few.

Far more so than many of our peers and almost all of our successors, we welcome the opportunity to tackle big issues and to draw on the concepts and tools of several disciplines. We remain broad synthesizers in a world of disciplinarians, all too often very narrow ones. And even those disciplinarians who may like or may even admire what we do have trouble defending our work to more tightly bound (or, less elegantly, more tight-assed) disciplinarians.

In so many ways, what I learned in Soc Rel has become the intellectual grounding for much of my subsequent work. Here's a relatively recent example. In the opening decades of this century, Katie Davis and I studied how young people were making use of the new digital media. We observed and studied many adolescents; we interviewed dozens of individuals who had worked with youth for at least twenty years; and we surveyed yet others, ranging from camp directors to psychoanalysts. When it came to putting our ideas together in book form, we decided to call the young people of today "the App Generation." We detailed how today's youth deal with their own sense of identity; how they negotiate intimate relations; and in which ways they are creative, imaginative, generative.

To the innocent reader, this would seem a standard work of social synthesis. But in fact, it built directly on the work of two teachers in Soc Rel who exerted powerful influences on me. When it came to speaking about this generation, we were comparing young people of today with those of earlier eras. This was a Riesmanian perspective, for social analyst David Riesman talked about colonists in the eighteenth century as traditional-directed, Americans in the nineteenth century as inner-directed, and citizens of the United States in the twentieth century as other-directed. Katie Davis and I were arguing that young people in the present century are best described as being "app-directed"—that they are powerfully (if unconsciously) affected by the apps available to them and the ways that those apps are typically used.

But if Riesman provided us a sociological lens, my tutor Erik Erikson provided a psychological lens. Erikson described a set of tensions that characterize different stages of life. The adolescent experiences a struggle between the desirable coalescence of identity and the risk of identity diffusion; the young adult experiences a struggle between the capacity for intimacy and the threat of isolation; and the maturing individual may turn out to be able to generate new ideas and relations, or, less happily, to be stuck in a rut. With respect to today's youth, we applied this Eriksonian lens to the elucidation of technologies that he could scarcely have imagined.

I believe that such studies are serious ones; over the last seventy years, many of us—including those who have not read their books—have learned an enormous amount from the kind of work carried out by scholars like Riesman and Erikson. But as I elaborate in the closing pages of this book, I believe it has been a mistake, perhaps a fatal arrogance, to call this endeavor *social science*. To be sure, we use scientific methods when possible and aspire to the status of science (former Harvard president Lawrence Summers once quipped, "Anything that calls itself a science isn't"). But we are not studying sciences in the same sense as physics or chemistry nor are we doing mathematics. For what we discover and can write about can also *change* what happens in the future—as I often put it, scholars like these can and have "changed the conversation."

I loved college. I took the courses I wanted to, made many new and good and long-lasting friends, had an enjoyable social life, and, with a talent that I have recently come to appreciate, found it easier than did most of my peers to form relations with professors. I audited so many courses in so many fields that I claimed to hold the record, though no one from the editorial staff of Guinness World Records has been keeping tabs. I joined study groups, where my friends and I talked about the "cepts"—the key terms in the field—and "the scoop"—the overall synthesis of the course. My unquenchable thirst for knowledge—a feature, indeed a gift, dating back to my earliest childhood—put me in good stead.

What of extracurricular activities, many of which I had pursued at Wyoming Seminary? In my freshman year, I elected not to compete for the school newspaper, the fabled *Harvard Crimson*, which was at the time a gateway to internships at prestigious newspapers and magazines. I made this decision for the perhaps ill-considered reason that I had edited the *Opinator* in high school and I believed there was no need to rehash the experience. Instead, I "comped" for the Crimson Key, an organization that gave, and still gives, tours of Harvard.

As with the choice of a literary history book for my Detur Prize, I am not sure of my motivations at the time. (In fact, my forehead wrinkles at the decisions made by a still young Howie, a name that stayed with me throughout college but was abruptly and permanently dropped thereafter.) I think it was in part because I was proud of being at Harvard, in part because I was able to earn a summer salary by giving tours. But it was also in part because, even before I failed to win the Wendell scholarship, I felt the need to develop my social skills, with other members of the Key and with the dozens, perhaps ultimately hundreds, of groups that I, walking backward most of the time, led around campus. (Without realizing it, I was also prepping for delivering talks to and answering questions from hundreds, maybe thousands, of collections of students and of audiences around the world in the ensuing decades.) Membership in the Key was fun but it was hardly transformative. Nor were other clubs and internships with which I had a loose affiliation over the years of college.

Yes, college was so enjoyable that I wished I could remain there forever. (And of course, in a sense I have succeeded in doing so!) In this wish, I was unusual. At both my college reunions and those attended by my wife Ellen (who attended Radcliffe College, part of Harvard, a few years later), I was surprised and disheartened to hear how many of my peers did *not* have positive memories of their four years in Cambridge, especially those who were women, minorities, or not heterosexual. I hope that more of today's graduates will have fond memories of their college years.

But four years are four years, and I knew that I had to make career decisions, or at the very least decide on "what's next." I was not explicitly aware of any expectations that I (and others) had for me. These expectations were finally explained to me, at the time of our fiftieth college reunion, by my classmate Nancy Chodorow, by then a well-known psychotherapist. "Howie," she exclaimed, "Don't you realize that Harvard has always been about one thing: *success*!" If I knew nothing else, I knew (at least in my Eriksonian unconscious) that Howie, in whom so many individuals, from family members to family friends to teachers and mentors, had invested so much, had better become successful . . . at something, anything.

An old joke: "What's a lawyer? A Jewish boy who hates the sight of blood." In fact, until my junior year, I considered only two careers: law and medicine. For medicine, I took biology and chemistry courses and worked for a while in an emergency room at nearby Mount Auburn Hospital. While in the Bay area during the summer after my junior year in college, I even met with Stanford Medical School's dean of admissions. But medicine as a profession never really attracted me. As for law, I took law professor's Paul Freund's famous course, The Legal Process (Soc Sci 137). I did well in the course, and Professor Freund suggested that I consider attending law school. I could see myself as a lawyer; I even realized that I seemed to have the "mind" of a lawyer. But back then, as now, I had little interest in defending clients who had probably committed misdeeds or in helping the wealthy become even wealthier. Public interest law was not on my radar; the term had barely been coined.

I wanted to tell myself, and to be able to tell my parents and relatives and family friends, that I *could* have been a standard Jewish professional, that I had the goods, so to speak. But my involvement with Soc Rel had done its job. Increasingly I saw myself as a future academic, one who would teach, do research, and publish, just like my dedicated tutors and admired professors were doing. (In a letter of recommendation that I happened to see, Professor Erikson described me succinctly as "research-oriented.") But in what subject, in what way, was not yet clear.

The work entailed in my senior thesis provides a clue as to where I was headed. I had the good fortune to have Professor Erikson as my tutor for two years. I was also able to persuade Charles (Chuck) Tilly, a distinguished sociologist, to serve as a co-tutor. Under their guidance, I carried out a prototypical Soc Rel thesis. Having secured funds, I spent the summer after my junior year studying a new and distinctly American phenomenon: *the retirement community*. Day after day I visited Leisure Village, a recently opened community restricted to individuals over the age of sixty in Vacaville, California, less than an hour's drive from Berkeley, where I was sharing an apartment on Dwight Way with a graduate student in engineering. I wrote a well-received thesis called "Gerontopia: Identity and Integrity in a Retirement Community."

The thesis was a reasonably proficient synthesis: recording what I had seen and heard (the journalist in me) and discussing it in terms of the then much-discussed concepts of identity, integrity, and community (the academic in me). I concluded that the various stakeholders each harbored their own dreams of what retirement could be like, and that these dreams invariably clashed—or as I would have put it more recently, their conceptions were "misaligned." For example, the community was completely split on whether grandchildren should be invited to enjoy or be prohibited from using the community swimming pool! My thesis was also a prototypical example of Soc Rel as an interdisciplinary field, synthesizing concepts and perspectives of psychology, sociology, and anthropology. Clearly, whether I knew it or not, this undergraduate was headed toward graduate studies in Soc Rel. The study had the potential to become a popular article or even a popular book. Some friends and mentors encouraged me to go in that direction, but I did not want to put additional work into my thesis once it had been handed in and graded.

But before I had to make a definitive decision about postgraduate studies, important detours loomed, two of which turned out to be life changing. The first detour was my receipt of a fellowship to spend a year anywhere in the then quite far-reaching British Commonwealth. Like many of my peers, I elected to go to London, where college friends would be in abundance, and where I could spend a year reading, writing, thinking, and taking advantage of the incredibly rich cultural life available in the mid-1960s. I probably attended more theater, concerts, and arts exhibitions in one year than in the succeeding decade. At the London School of Economics, I had a wonderful tutor, Ernest Gellner, a self-described social anthropologist and philosopher, who could easily have been mistaken for a prototypical Soc Rel faculty member. I also had the opportunity to travel throughout Europe and to the Soviet Union. In the lingo of French sociologist, Pierre Bourdieu, I was accumulating substantial amounts of social and cultural capital—perhaps even enough to compete with greater chances someday as a successor to the Wendell fellowship!

But I still needed to decide what to do at the end of my fellowship. Very much under the wing of Professor Erikson, and admiring his clinical powers, but not wanting to go through medical school (Erikson himself had never even gone to college), I applied and was accepted to doctoral programs in clinical psychology—the shorter route to clinical practice in the psychoanalytic mode. But my heart was not in it, and when a second opportunity arose—through a chance hitched ride to Ann Arbor, Michigan, to visit a graduate program at the university there—I quickly, and with little regret, abandoned those plans. In the process of dropping these plans, I disappointed those who had supported my interest in clinical psychology. Over fifty years later, I still feel a twinge of guilt, as I don't like to disappoint expectations of myself or of others.

On that fateful hitched ride, I learned that a noted psychology professor at Harvard, Jerome Bruner, had launched an imaginative educational intervention for students in the middle grades of elementary school. Professor Bruner was looking for research assistants to work on "Man: A Course of Study" or MACOS, an interdisciplinary introduction for ten-year-olds to the field of psychology and other social sciences—indeed, an elementary school version of Soc Rel!

On the suggestion of the driver, I went to see Professor Bruner. In a manner reminiscent of a movie director casting a minor role in a forthcoming film, Bruner talked to me for a few minutes, and then said, "Go work out details with Annette Kaysen [his able assistant] and we'll see you at the Underwood School in Newton in two weeks." And there went my future career as a clinical psychologist.

Though psychology was part of the Soc Rel disciplinary trio, I had never actually taken a course in what the academy deems to call "psychology." My psychology-inflected courses were in psychoanalysis of the Eriksonian stripe, appropriate perhaps for those who wanted to be psychiatrists or clinicians but not for those who wanted to be "real" experimental psychologists. Bruner himself had been trained in social as well as physiological psychology—hence his association over time with both the Soc Rel and the psychology departments. But more significantly, he had since become one of the founders of a new field called *cognitive psychology*: the study of how the mind reasons, both when it is working well and when it is distorted or distended or even destroyed in various ways. (Twenty years later I wrote the first history of the broader field called cognitive science, and dubbed it *The Mind's New Science*.)

This excursion into the preparation of a course for young students turned out to be a perfect coda to my college experience. I loved learning about cognition, and especially about the observational and empirical work on cognitive development: how the minds of children change on the basis of seemingly preprogrammed steps but also in light of their playful and more focused explorations, both formal and informal. I had scarcely heard of Jean Piaget, but was fascinated to learn about his groundbreaking observations of his own three children and his large-scale, more experimental studies of how, over the course of time and in light of their actions in the world, children develop logical thinking, social thinking, and moral thinking. I could see myself carrying out such studies. As an Eagle Scout and a sometime piano teacher I had always enjoyed interacting with children and trying to understand what made them tick.

But this summer's work under Bruner's curation was not "school as usual." With generous funding but also with strict deadlines, my colleagues and I were developing the aforementioned curriculum "Man: A Course of Study." The three guiding questions of the curriculum have remained until today as "frontlets between my eyes": What makes human beings human? How did they get that way?

How could they be made more human? In retrospect, I realize that these are prototypical synthesizing questions. One can approach them only if one is open to material from several disciplines and sources of knowledge, and also is willing, playfully yet determinedly, to put them together in ways that make some sense for those involved—be they professors, middle school teachers, recent college graduates, or, if we were fortunate, ten-year-olds taking a summer course in Newton, Massachusetts (who were necessarily predisciplinary). A daily exercise for synthesizing minds!

My job, as a member of the just formed "instructional research group" or IRG, was to help design lessons each day, observe how they worked (or did not work) with fifth graders, and then both revise the day's lessons and plan the next day's lesson. I liked this work and was good enough at it. All of the half-dozen or so individuals who made up the IRG were engaged each day in enjoyable and high-stakes synthesizing of the content, observing how it was working, and deciding what changes could and should be made in the following hours. At the time, I had not heard of management consulting firms like McKinsey, but I suspect that the focus and pace of MACOS was in certain respects similar to the experience of a team visiting a site on the fly and trying to figure out just what those working at the site should be doing.

What made an even greater impression on me was how Jerry (for, by that time, we all called him Jerry) ran his operation. There was scarcely any hierarchy other than one focused on the quality of one's ideas and how effectively one presented and defended them and, as needed, revised or even withdrew them. From esteemed professors and consultants, to classroom teachers, to lowly research assistants, we all ate together in the basement of the Underwood School, where delicatessen food was brought in each noon by two high school students who used their parents' station wagons. On many evenings, we were welcomed to Jerry and Blanche Bruner's spacious home on Follen Street near Harvard Square, where we rubbed elbows with some of the leading thinkers and practitioners of the era—again, with scarcely any regard to status. Without being cognizant of it, I was acquiring knowledge about one way to lead and, if one were fortunate, perhaps to inspire a research group. And though I only became aware of it more recently, I even copied the dress and certain mannerisms of this charismatic and entrepreneurial scholar.

This unanticipated experience in the summer of 1965 also influenced my life and career aspirations. At the start of the summer, I was a recent college graduate who was unexcited about a future career as a clinical psychologist. By the end of the summer, I was about to go abroad on my post-college fellowship; I was well on the road to applying to a doctoral program in developmental psychology (organizationally, part of Soc Rel at Harvard), à la Bruner and Piaget; and I had fallen in love with another member of the Bruner team, Judith (Judy) Krieger, who had already been admitted to the doctoral program in developmental psychology at Harvard. A year later, following my year abroad, Judy and I were married, and I had begun my doctoral studies in developmental psychology—a field unknown to me during my four years of college.

4

RESISTING A SINGLE FRAME

Much as I loved my four years in college, I disliked, even loathed graduate school. May I count the ways?

To begin with, I did not resonate much with my classmates or with several of the key faculty, nor they with me. Nowadays, we might say that we simply did not click. No blame either way.

Then I discovered that I was not that enamored of experimental psychology, the approach to research taken—then as now—in the subfields of developmental and social psychology. The field typically entailed the construction and facile use of testing mechanical or electronic apparatus (and I was not facile in mastering its use); fastidious planning of the procedure or intervention step by step; and collecting mountains of data directly related to a prior, explicitly stated hypothesis; and then analyzing it and, as needed, reanalyzing over and over again before declaring a finding and reaching a conclusion. No way did I see myself doing that for the rest of my working life! In contrast, many of my classmates and some of my professors had come out of (and perhaps had escaped from) the "harder sciences" like chemistry or biology; they were used to the milestones and millstones, as well as the rhythms and occasional thrills, of lab work. It was not even clear that they particularly liked children, or human beings in general, but regarded them more as "research subjects."

Then in the first weeks of graduate school, a most unpleasant incident occurred. I was taking the required "pro-seminar" in social psychology, taught by two youngish professors. Tom Pettigrew was an expert in race relations, and Stanley Milgram was a clever experimentalist as well as a brilliant conceptualizer.

Milgram was garnering acclaim for his studies on obedience to authority. Countering the prediction that he had garnered from experts in the field, Milgram demonstrated that ordinary individuals, when so instructed by a scientist wearing a white coat in a laboratory setting, would deliver apparently painful shocks—up to a clearly dangerous level—to another ordinary individual. (The apparent recipient of the shock was a confederate of the experimenter, and painful shocks were not actually being administered.) These experiments were widely interpreted as evidence that most of us, if so directed by an apparently authoritative figure, would inflict harm on others. The implication was that nearly all of us have the potential to become "obedient Nazis."

I had nothing against Milgram and nothing against the studies, which I found fascinating. But in class I dared to raise a few questions—perhaps somewhat challenging but not meant to be disrespectful—to Professor Milgram.

What followed was shocking in another sense. Milgram lashed out at me as if I were a bomb thrower—attacking me, belittling me, asserting that I was trying to "destroy" him. It was behavior, or more precisely *misbehavior*, that was totally out of place in a sedate graduate seminar filled with brand new students. As surprising as Milgram's unwarranted attack on me was what did *not* ensue. Neither his colleague Professor Pettigrew nor any of the twenty or so others in the seminar room rose to my defense or attempted to defuse the attack. Only after the class was over did others, including Professor Pettigrew, come over to console me.

To this day I do not know whether Milgram had simply "lost it" or whether he was actually conducting some kind of informal experiment to see how I would react. (Nowadays, neither the original Milgram study nor such an ad hoc attack would be permitted by the committee in charge of studies involving human subjects.) But this initially traumatic experience turned out to be instructive: I learned that in academia, as in other spheres, you can be attacked without reason and quite viciously, and you cannot count on others to defend you. At the same time, the experience helped me to develop a thicker skin. Subsequent attacks on my scholarly work or on me, much milder to be sure, have not bothered me that much.

Milgram and I never discussed the incident again. Instead, we assumed the normal professor-student relation. He even read and commented helpfully on subsequent papers. Unlike Pettigrew, Milgram did not get tenure at Harvard, and I have often wondered whether his pugnacious and volatile personality was a factor. Milgram went on to have a distinguished career, cut tragically short by a heart attack at the age of fifty-one. I have long since forgiven his outburst, though I remain mystified by the incident. Today a student so attacked might well file a formal complaint (in fact, nowadays, such an incident might even be surreptitiously recorded on a cell phone!). Such responses would not have occurred to my classmates and me at the time. I think that the present trend is a good thing, but I am not absolutely certain that it is.

I could not help contrasting my undergraduate experiences at Harvard College with my graduate school experiences at Harvard University, in the very same (then new and in my view quite hideous) building, William James Hall (WJH). As an undergraduate, I was free to take what I liked, to explore new topics and unfamiliar disciplines, to put forth increasingly adventurous syntheses, to form friendships in the dorms, to be courted by faculty members who wanted to attract and even inspire committed students and potential acolytes.

In contrast, as a doctoral student, in the very same department of Social Relations, I clearly inhabited the lowest rung on the academic totem pole. Faculty were interested in pursuing their own research, in securing research grants and piling on publications and, if fortunate, in receiving accolades of various sorts—more likely from distant lands than from across the hallway. Getting to the top of the discipline and remaining there was a prepotent motivator: these acclaimed scholars were also in fierce competition with one another.

Lest you doubt my characterization, consider this situation. In the late 1960s, WJH housed four research laboratories whose "principal investigators" worked with infants: in the basement, on the fifth floor, the eleventh floor, and the fourteenth floor. Students who worked in one lab were discouraged, if not forbidden, from working in other labs, and some professors made them in effect take oaths of silence—or "nondisclosure agreements," in the current parlance. Professors wanted us to be widgets in their labs, and, though I did not think of myself as particularly proud or arrogant, I was not interested in being a cog in *anyone's* machinery. Some years later, I observed that the students who landed the best *initial* jobs were ones who had been the best widgets as doctoral students, but in most cases not the ones who ultimately went on to change the field or the conversation. Being a widget does not easily translate into being a wizard.

Perhaps I can best distinguish these contrasting experiences by invoking two educational models. When I was an undergraduate, I was able to have mentors who took a personal interest in my development and who opened me up to their respective worlds. In the case of Erik Erikson, he invited me to come to his office on a regular basis, asked for my opinion about materials he was reading or thinking about, and even invited my classmates and me to his modest home for a barbecue. As already mentioned, in our intensive summer devoted to the development of educational materials, Jerry Bruner paid little attention to status and, again, opened up his home on a regular basis to the lowly as well as the high-and-mighty.

To elaborate on a point made earlier: mentoring relationships contain a duality. The mentee is searching for a senior figure with whom he or she identifies, learns from, and hopes someday to emulate. As a child, my parents and my Uncle Fritz were my principal role models. Once I went to college, my professors—nearly all male, many of them Jewish, some of them of escapees from Nazi Europe—assumed that role. But mentorship involves a dual recognition. In taking on mentees, the mentor often discerns characteristics that resonate. The mentor hopes that the mentee will one day carry on some of the work of the mentor, and perhaps even in the way that the mentor would have executed it. Certainly, that's been the case with me in the ensuing decades, as I have evolved into the roles of mentor and even grand-mentor.

There is no reason why such mentor–mentee relationships can't occur in graduate work or even in postdoctoral work. In fact they do, and Nelson Goodman, to be introduced shortly, played that role in my own life. But they are perhaps less likely in general, because the focus at this stage falls on professionalization, with apprentice–master as the obvious model. In any event, it did not occur with respect to my own graduate work—and perhaps, because I can appear judgmental or confrontational vis-à-vis others (recall my clash with Miss Dyer, way back in sixth grade), I was at least partly to blame.

Putting it all together, I have termed my stance "resisting professionalization." Or perhaps "refusing to be disciplined by *any* discipline." What our professors were trying to do as researchers— mostly appropriately, even though I believe I could have helped some of them to do it more effectively and more appealingly—I did not easily see myself doing. And certainly not for the rest of my active work life! I did not want to *be trained* in experimental psychology; nor did I want to *train others* in that line of work. I wanted to continue the exploratory adventure of my college years, or, though I would not have then been able to formulate it in these words, I wanted to synthesize broadly in one area or topic and then move on to another quite different one. Now, toward the end of what has been a long and good life, I can say with gratitude (and heaving a sigh of relief), that's what I have been able to do, more or less.

But back to the late 1960s: What to do? (Or to echo Vladimir Lenin, "What is to be done?") Being methodical, I sat down and made a list of pros and cons: why should I stay in graduate school instead of, say, going to law school and, alternatively, why should I leave? The list was pretty evenly split. In the end, the scale tipped toward remaining because of an insight: I could ignore as much as possible the things that I did not like, while taking advantage of the graduate school opportunities (at that time, fully paid for by government scholarships) to do what *I wanted to do in the way I wanted to do it.* Again, I have been more fortunate than most in having had that opportunity. Once having made the decision, it was not that hard to ignore people with whom I did not resonate, to avoid initiation rites in which I did not wish to participate, and, echoing a quite different figure, Frank Sinatra, to do it "my way."

Being married to my fellow graduate student Judy, beginning a family, and having friends from college nearby in other professional schools all helped. Finally, I found an adviser, Professor Roger Brown, an expert in social psychology as well as in the study of language, whom I cherished and who seemed to like me. Roger allowed me to do what I wanted to do, supported me, defended me against other professors who were critical of me (one of whom clearly wanted to kick me out of the program), and ultimately helped me to win coveted fellowships.

Acknowledging the passage of time, it's important to note two big differences between 1965 and 2020. First, most of my Harvard College classmates and I chose professional callings in which we remained for the rest of our lives. In my case, of my dozen closest college friends, ten remained in the career for which they were initially trained, largely in the professions. Second, almost everyone who graduated from college with high honors, as I did, went on to receive doctorates and most became professors. Today, the sirenic lures of Wall Street, Hollywood, and Silicon Valley are so patent and so seductive, in terms of both salary and lifestyle, that I worry that we in "the academy" will not be able to nurture and retain those college students who could become outstanding professors in the future. And even when a recipient of a doctorate is fortunate enough to secure a reasonable position as a teacher and scholar, the life of a professor is less attractive today, except at the most selective and well-resourced schools.

So there I was in graduate school, enjoying some courses, topics, and professors, disliking others, but mostly champing at the bit to get out, to break free—though just what I would do thereafter was less certain. After all, I would be happy to become a professor, but I did not see myself as a professor of experimental psychology. And Soc Rel, already on life support, would be pronounced dead within a year after I received my doctorate.

Then I encountered another one of those chance events that can, for better or worse, change one's life. I was taking a doctoral seminar from Sheldon White, a "dust bowl"-trained experimental child psychologist who had evolved into something of a grand theorist. In passing, Professor White mentioned that Nelson Goodman, professor of philosophy at nearby Brandeis University, was thinking of moving to Harvard. Goodman planned to start a research project in the arts and was looking for research assistants. Fortunately I had heard of Goodman and knew that he was an eminent epistemologist, though I doubt that I had read any of his books and did not quite understand why, in particular, he would want to move to the Graduate School of Education at Harvard and launch a research project. In the spring of 1967, I made the trek to the Brandeis campus in Waltham, Massachusetts, and had what turned out to be a "job interview" with this formidable intellect. Professor Goodman even *looked* smarter than the rest of us, with a high forehead and a clear-eyed penetrating stare, his fingers drumming somewhat aggressively and ominously on the otherwise spare table (see his photo in the first group of photos).

I got off on the wrong foot. In response to a question about my familiarity with philosophy, I mentioned that I had been reading the work of Maurice Merleau-Ponty, a French phenomenologist. Goodman frowned noticeably. But then, when I added that I had also been reading the work of Susanne Langer, a philosopher of the arts (who had been the college teacher of my wife Judy), Professor Goodman visibly relaxed and said "Well, that's another story." That brief conversation changed my life—one of those positive transformational experiences.

Though he had spent his academic career at the University of Pennsylvania and Brandeis University, Goodman, a native of the Boston area, was yet another Harvard academic, having received both his bachelor's (1928) and his doctoral degrees (1941) there. He was eager to return to Harvard and, at long last, Harvard seemed ready to welcome him back to its ranks.

Accordingly, in the fall of 1967, at the Harvard Graduate School of Education (HGSE), Nelson Goodman launched Harvard Project Zero (PZ). He hired me, as well as David Perkins, then a graduate student in mathematics and artificial intelligence at MIT, as the first research assistants on the project. Though at Harvard since 1961 I had rarely set foot in HGSE.[1] Unlike Soc Rel, Project Zero has turned out to be a very useful name—as we old-timers like to say, *it reveals nothing.*

---

1. At the time, the main building at the "Ed school," Longfellow Hall, on loan from Radcliffe College, had no urinals!

In addition to being a first-class epistemologist, Goodman was also enamored of the arts. He collected paintings, drawings, and sculpture; he had run an art gallery in Boston for fifteen years; he was married to a well-known visual artist, Katherine Sturgis; and he was completing a major treatise on the nature and the epistemology of artistic knowledge called *Languages of Art*, a book quite close in spirit—though not at all in philosophical argot—to Susanne Langer's *Philosophy in a New Key*.

In *Languages of Art* (which we at PZ soon nicknamed "The Bible"), Goodman set out a rigorous typology of the variety of symbols and symbol systems employed in various art forms. In a single paragraph in the concluding pages, Goodman mused about whether scholars and researchers could accumulate "systematic knowledge" on how individuals become involved in and may ultimately master various art forms. He conceded that there is plenty of reasonable lore about artistic education in studios, ateliers, backstage conversations, and stage whispers. But he lamented that this knowledge was anecdotal and impressionistic. If one wanted to develop systematic knowledge, in the manner of a serious researcher, one had effectively to *start at zero*.

In addition to Dave Perkins and me, Goodman gathered around him a group of mostly young students from a range of disciplines (music, visual arts, architecture, theater, psychology, computer science, to name a few), and a few professor friends, and asked them to join forces with him on this intellectual and organizational adventure. A prototypical interdisciplinary team! Initially we were unpaid—a tradition, I like to joke, that we have happily continued for over half a century. (In fact, researchers at PZ do get paid, though not very much.) Goodman ran the project for a few years and then said to Dave Perkins and me, "Well, fellows, if you want to run it, it's yours."

We were not quite aware of it at the time, but Goodman simply meant that, henceforth, Dave and I would have to raise the money to cover salaries, research materials, travel expenses, technological needs, and space. To everyone's surprise, including our own, we were able to rise to the occasion. Dave and I codirected the project for twenty-eight years, and one of my proudest achievements is that, at the time of this writing, PZ is more active and vigorous than it has ever been. Nelson, who died in 1998 at the age of ninety-two, would be bemused and amused, but also secretly proud. As he might have put it in his arch way, "In the end Zero has added up to something."[2]

Project Zero and Nelson Goodman gave me two very important gifts: a role model for scholarly work and leadership, and the beginnings of a scholarly project that I (and many others) would continue to pursue for many years.

While Goodman and Jerry Bruner were friends and remained in contact with one another for many years, they could not have been more different in personality. In the late 1960s, Goodman ran the nascent research project on artistic knowledge quite differently from the way Bruner ran the curriculum development project a few years earlier. Goodman was far more hierarchical, far less expansive in personal contacts (Bruner was a prototypical extrovert, Goodman essentially an introvert), and a far more judgmental adviser.

---

2. I describe what it takes for a research institute to survive in a university setting in https://howardgardner.com/2019/08/12/how-institutions-survive -and-sometimes-thrive-a-challenge-to-ralph-waldo-emerson/.

Bruner alighted upon what was exciting and moved on, often at breakneck speed, to the next point, whereas Goodman focused sharply on what was wrong or infelicitous and lingered there. In a comment that haunts me almost every day—especially as I am writing—Goodman said, "When I read something, as soon as I come to a line that does not make sense, I stop reading." Whatever rigor may mark my thinking and writing should be credited largely to Nelson.

But Goodman's intellectual style nicely complemented Bruner's. While Bruner moved—some would say, flitted—from one topic to another, Nelson stuck on something until he got it absolutely right. Without realizing at the time, I was getting for free a graduate course in strict philosophical argument. Renowned British intellectual historian Isaiah Berlin famously divided scholars into two types: the fox knows many little things, the hedgehog knows one big thing. Nelson once quipped "I know *one* little thing." Of course, he was a giant in what he knew. We might say that Goodman had a prototypical disciplinary mind—he was a philosophers' philosopher—and that Bruner had a prototypical synthesizing mind—he was a synthesizer's synthesizer. But with their stature as scholars and their status in life, they were both open to disciplinary (philosophy and psychology, respectively) and interdisciplinary synthesizing work, thus making them ideal teachers for me. And perhaps because neither was my doctoral adviser—I was fortunate that Roger Brown agreed to assume that role—Goodman and Bruner may have felt less of a need to discipline me in the way that they were presumably disciplining their own students. In a sense, I was more of an undergraduate mentee than an aspiring disciplinarian stuck somewhere in the pipeline. I also benefited from what I later termed "frag-mentoring": the opportunity to emulate particular aspects of particular mentors.

I would like to think that, in the research teams that I have assembled and led—including the team that helped me to develop the theory of multiple intelligences—I made symbiotic use of the intellectual leadership traits that I observed in these two wonderful mentors, who could not have been more different from one another. Both Goodman and Bruner cared enough to nurture me; both took a paternal interest in me; and, as we aged, I took on a caring "filial" relationship to each of them. If I heeded or blended their respective lessons well, I could retain in scholarly work my penchant for broad interdisciplinary syntheses with a greater precision in argumentation.

Personality also plays a role here. As mentioned, Bruner had an expansive personality; he was a natural extrovert and loved to engage others. Goodman was clearly introverted; he hated small talk and loved to spend hours alone with art objects. Someone once told me that I am a "compensated introvert," a combination of my introverted father and my extroverted mother, and the prototypical "connector"—though no one in my experience could match my mother's skill at making human connections. That seems about right to me.

In addition to contributing to my intellectual style, Goodman also helped me to discern what became my distinctive first lines of work as a budding scholar. Basically, he allowed me to put together, to synthesize, two interests of mine in a way that was unusual, if not unprecedented.

On one side was my long-term interest in the arts. I had been a pianist for two decades, and, especially as a result of undergraduate courses and my year of accumulating "culture credits" in England, I had become an aficionado of the arts. I wanted to understand the various arts, their relationship to one another, and their distinctive contributions. In terms that I borrowed from Susanne Langer and Nelson Goodman, I wanted to understand *how their respective symbol systems*—words, images, notes, dance steps—*work*. Like many others of the day, I saw the arts as a privileged home for creativity. As a beginning doctoral student, I even wrote a fifty-page treatise on the psychological study of creativity, and received relevant feedback from my one-time *bête noir*, Stanley Milgram (which in my development as a scholar helped convert Milgram from a tor-mentor to a frag-mentor).

On the other hand was my newly emerging focal interest in cognitive development, from infancy to adulthood. This line of study, and whatever experimental and analytic tools I was acquiring in graduate school, grew out of the work of two scholarly giants of the field, Jean Piaget and Jerome Bruner. To be sure, both of these master psychologists had some personal interest in the arts. But for them, as for almost every other scholar in William James Hall and in the broader psychological research community around the globe, *development meant thinking logically, like a scientist*—thinking like Piaget, Bruner, and others who shared the scientific ambitions of an emerging field like Soc Rel.

One day I had a stimulating though eccentric thought: *What would happen if I combined these two interests?* More specifically, what would happen if I took the concepts and tools of cognitive developmental psychology, as honed by my teachers, and applied them instead to artistic thinking, skill, creativity, and the like? Put a bit more technically, could I create a "cognitive psychology of artistic development" to set alongside the comparatively well established "cognitive psychology of scientific development"? Perhaps indeed, to anticipate a phrase that I would not have used at the time, is there a difference, are there differences, between "artistic" and "scientific" intelligences? (The short answer: any intelligence *can* be used artistically, but that's an option, not a requirement.)

This promising idea became my project and a major thrust of PZ in the ensuing decade. On the experimental side, my colleagues and I conducted empirical studies of how children develop key artistic capacities. We studied how they perceive style in painting, for example, and in later studies, how they perceive style in other art forms like music and literature. Our research team also studied an important kind of artistic cognition that entailed the creation and comprehension of metaphor. Metaphoric thought is clearly fundamental both in making connections and in capturing those connections in some kind of symbol system, linkages essential for many types of synthesis. On this basis, I launched a real if modest line of empirical research, and also found ways to support this line of research through securing government and private philanthropic funding.

You may wonder, given my lack of enthusiasm about experimental studies, how I went about these psychological studies. They were not bereft of hypotheses, but the hypotheses were quite soft-spoken. Without being conscious of it, I was trying to open up new fields of study. Do children recognize style in works of art? Are they sensitive to metaphors, and, if so, of what types, and under what conditions? As in so much of my subsequent empirical work, the more interesting hypotheses arose as a *consequence* of this initial experimentation. They were the results, rather than the motivators, of the initial studies. Is recognition of an artist's style helped or hindered by the inclusion of subject matter—for example, is it easier to recognize style in figurative or in abstract paintings? Do we process physical metaphors and psychological metaphors in similar or distinctive ways? In both cases I initiated a small cottage industry of studies on these topics: the development of thinking, problem solving, and problem finding in the arts.

In a chapter dedicated to the dissection of professionalization, I'll relate a brief but telling aside. I carried out a groundbreaking study on children's sensitivity to painting styles. Unlike most doctoral students, I was not working under supervision in the lab of an experimental psychologist—what I might now term "the Germanic master–pupil academic model." Therefore, as a solitary scholarly entrepreneur, I had to "sell" the resulting paper myself. I first showed it to the wife and lab manager of a distinguished (and personally difficult) psychophysicist, S. S. Stevens. "Didi" Stevens glanced at it and said, with more than a trace of dismissiveness, "Smitty would have no interest in this," and handed it back to me. If rejections are going to take place, it is best if they take place quickly and decisively, I guess.

I then sent the paper to the editor of another journal, *Psychonomic Science* (I don't know how one comes up with such an infelicitous title). The editor Clifford Morgan politely rejected it by return mail. (Again, best if the rejection occurs quickly.) But just some months later, the same journal accepted and published an article by a well-known psychologist Richard Walk—on essentially the same subject! Quite annoyed, and never a shrinking violet (again recalling my mother's confrontation of my elementary school principal about the misbehavior of my teacher), I dispatched a letter of protest to

Morgan and said, in effect, "How dare you reject my article and then proceed to accept Dr. Walk's?"

Again, I got a quick response. In psychology, wrote Morgan, we *do* "concept formation." We don't *do* "artistic style"—that's for a journal in aesthetics. This is the kind of lesson that a traditional mentor could have readily told me, but I had to learn it for myself. My adviser Roger Brown mollified my hurt feelings, saying, "We all have manila folders labeled 'unpublished papers.'" I have often used this expression with my own students: part of being a scholar is developing a skin thick enough to deal with rejections and with "revise and resubmit" feedback that often engenders much unneeded work.

So that was me (by then, everyone called me Howard) as a tradesperson, an apprentice in the execution and promulgation of research in cognitive development, a novice in the world of academic publishing. But I also had grander aspirations, and I began to think in earnest about what it would take to develop a whole developmental psychology of the arts.

I could have written an article about this idea, but I realized that it was really a task for a book. Accordingly, I sketched out a grandiose work that came to be entitled *The Arts and Human Development*. In that book, still in print the last time I looked, I reviewed the available literature—in English, French, and German—and tried to lay out a complete scheme of artistry, one that rivaled what others were well along in creating with respect to the development of scientific cognition. The work was undeniably a work of synthesis— putting together many strands of information—but in a framework that others had not considered, and so it had at least a pretense to creativity as well. I dare to think it was also ahead of its time. We now have forty years of research on topics broached there, most of that research carried out by people who have likely not heard of me or of the book. (Frankfurt, Germany, now has an entire Max Planck Institute devoted to "empirical aesthetics"). In ways I could never have anticipated, this novel attempt at synthesizing served as a model for *Frames of Mind*, my major work on intelligence and intelligences that was to emerge a decade later, and of other book length synoptic works as well.

A senior colleague once remarked about *The Arts and Human Development*: "It's the book of a very young scholar." This was meant as a critical barb, but with the passage of time, I'll accept the comment as perceptive: the book could have been written much more clearly, with less dense terminology, more evident headlines and takeaways.

A related thought: In later life the renowned economist John Kenneth Galbraith thought back to his first books, wrapped in scholarly jargon and addressed to the small field of scholars in the appropriate subdisciplines. The books sold poorly and were soon remaindered. Galbraith learned his lesson. He resolved that in future, everything he had to say, he would say in clear English so that his books would sell so well and be so widely known that his colleagues in the economics trade would *have to read them* in order to respond appropriately when queried about them at cocktail parties or on a train ride.

As a doctoral student I worked on other book-length projects. In the process I was gaining familiarity with the operation of the literary marketplace. Eric Valentine of Wiley Publishers told me that he could offer an advance of $1,500 for *The Arts and Human Development* because that's what the sales force estimated the book would recoup. Drawing on what I had learned from my business-man father and my uncle Fritz, I replied that I would not settle for that advance; I wanted an advance of \$3,000. Shortly afterward Eric Valentine got back to me and said, "We redid the figures and we can offer you \$3,000." While I am scarcely a bargainer of Trumpian conceit, I learned that as a scholar, one does have a certain degree of leverage when dealing with the dreaded though essential world of commerce.

What of the other books? They could not have been more differ-ent. To make money one summer, I responded to an ad looking for help in writing a textbook. The man who had placed the ad was a social psychologist, Martin Grossack, who wanted to write a text-book but had run into a problem—presumably writer's block. Marty was a nice fellow, but it became clear that he was not going to finish his undertaking; indeed he had barely begun. He needed a writer, disguised as a researcher.

As it happens I had just completed the required introduction to social psychology, the course cotaught by Milgram and Pettigrew. And so I was up-to-date, at least as much as current professors at Harvard who were surveying the field. Once I had signed on with Marty Grossack and gauged the problem, I became the ghost writer. Most of the topics, and virtually all of the words, were mine. I might have been content to just take the money and run, but Grossack realized that was not quite fair and so he put my name on the book—second, of course. The book was a rather standard textbook, in which I did what I had been good at since high school: summariz-ing topics and putting them into a comfortable, inviting framework.

What would raise eyebrows today are the title and the cover illus-tration. Hold onto your seat: with the subtitle "Social Psychology as

Social Science" the book was called *Man and Men*. And the cover featured silhouettes of men, presumably all Caucasian (it's reproduced in the first group of photos). As shocking as the name and illustration seem today is the fact that, as far as I can remember, no one objected to either instantiation. Such was the state of things in the academy of the late 1960s.

The book was probably important chiefly because it demonstrated that I could write a textbook and get it published. *I was a reliable and accessible summarizer or synthesizer and an adequate if not vivid and evocative writer.* Nearly all of my peers in graduate programs in psychology around the country were in labs, carrying out experiments and writing short, empirical (and all too often unreadable) scholarly articles, poised for submission initially to the journals with the greatest prestige. Here I was, alone at my desk, reading articles and books, and putting them together in a reader-friendly, book-length format. A decade later, I succeeded in writing a textbook of my own in developmental psychology, one that was quite original and surprisingly successful. Indeed, if my life had taken another turn, I could have made a reasonable living revising that text and generating other texts. I am so pleased that, thanks to an unexpected financial boon (see page 125), my life did not need to take that alluring but unsatisfying turn toward mammon. Synthesizing the words and the works of others did not suffice.

Before I get to the third book, let me mention how I was spending time when I was not carrying out research, banging out workaday prose on the typewriters of the day, or doing my share of housework and child rearing (some, but certainly less than half). In a word, I was teaching. To begin with, in a very modest way, I continued to teach piano. But now it was no longer chiefly about picking up spare change. Rather, since I was trying to understand artistic development, I reflected on various teaching techniques and took notes about what worked and what did not: the empirical psychology of artistic pedagogy (though fortunately I never wrote anything with such a pretentious and off-putting a title).

Then, in a move that was, again, quite unusual for doctoral students, I decided to teach in the public schools. My reasoning was that if I were going to spend my life as an expert in developmental psychology, I should not just observe children (including my own) or carry out experiments on those whose parents permitted them to participate in research, I should actually try to teach something to a group of youngsters. And so for several months, I was one of two teachers of a K–2 class at the Underwood School, the same school in nearby Newton where Bruner and company had developed Man: A Course of Study, just a few years earlier.

Third, and most important, I myself became a tutor—a teacher of Harvard College undergraduates in Soc Rel. I had been affiliated with Winthrop House as an undergraduate, but now became a tutor in nearby Quincy House. And for three years, I taught undergraduates the basic texts and ideas in sociology, anthropology, and various strands of psychology. While probably not a natural teacher—I am too introverted and live too much in my own mind—I became reasonably proficient. And I realized that if I were to become a teacher, I should teach my own topics, interests, disciplines, and skills (especially writing skills) to college or graduate students, and not to toddlers. I lacked the skills of teaching young children, other than those in my own growing family, nor did I have the motivation to acquire those skills.

As a tutor in Quincy House, I got to rub elbows with well-known figures, including poet Robert Lowell and political-scientist-turned-senator Daniel Patrick Moynihan. I was also in charge of inviting distinguished guests to come to Harvard College and speak to students. We did not offer an honorarium (in those days colleges and universities rarely did), but we did cover basic expenses.

Many well-known figures accepted the invitation. I remember particularly Noam Chomsky, the linguist and social critic, who was becoming a national figure and who is today undoubtedly the most eminent public intellectual in the world. I remember pollster Louis Harris, who on his own initiative stayed at the luxury Boston Ritz hotel and asked us to cover the costs of both his wife and himself—not a wild request, but one of which I did not approve. And with vividness, I remember Rudolf Bing, the formidable head of the Metropolitan Opera. About sixty years old, he arrived with an attractive young woman, who could not have been more than half his age, and clearly not his wife. I was so naive in those days that this shocked me. Just as when, in October 1963, Professor Galbraith walked through the lunch line at Winthrop House with actress Angie Dickinson at his side, it never occurred to me that she was awaiting president John F. Kennedy, who arrived on campus shortly thereafter.

The rejections of my perhaps sophomoric invitations to luminaries to spend a few hours at Quincy House with students and faculty were equally informative, and perhaps even more memorable. In his own grand scrawl, novelist and essayist Gore Vidal explained that he was too involved in the forthcoming national election (of 1968) and that he would get back to me after the election. (As far as I recall, he never did.) I also invited legendary comedian Groucho

Marx and he sent back a letter that was inimitably Groucho. (See the letter in the first photo section.)

Finally, I invited my personal intellectual hero Edmund "Bunny" Wilson, the literary critic of broad but impressively deep knowledge of a wide range of topics. As I mentioned earlier, since my college days, he had been my role model as a thinker, writer, and master synthesizer, and one who had deliberately chosen not to spend significant amounts of time in the academy. Which, as he wisely discerned, would try to discipline him—shades of "Huck Finn."

Not surprisingly, I received one of Wilson's trademarks declinations, "Edmund Wilson regrets that he is unable to . . ." with a check mark next to "give talks." I saved the envelope from the Wilson note, often wondering whether he himself had addressed the envelope. Years later, when one could look at samples of handwriting on a search engine, I called up Wilson's script and sure enough (I happen to be a skilled amateur in graphology—a story for my *personal* memoir!), the great Wilson had himself addressed the envelope. While it would have been a "high" to meet and listen to Wilson on almost any topic (despite an apparent stammer), I cherish this handcrafted rejection (see the photograph in the first group of photos).

On to the third book, which proved to be the most important from the point of view of my subsequent career. Ever since I had worked with Bruner in the summer of 1965 and had my intellectual horizons greatly broadened, I had been fascinated by two scholars of French background: Jean Piaget, pioneer researcher in cognitive development from Geneva (in the French-speaking part of Switzerland); and Claude Lévi-Strauss, Parisian anthropologist who adopted a cognitive stance toward various cultural entities and artifacts—a stance emanating from the study of language as carried out by linguists of the time, most notably Roman Jakobson.

During my year in Europe, I read extensively in the works of both professors, both in English and, dictionary in hand, in French. I also made it a point to meet Piaget in Geneva and to attend a lecture by Lévi-Strauss in London. While both scholars were quite well-known in their respective fields, the relationship between their works had not been discerned and dissected, so far as I could determine

After musing about the connections between Piaget and Lévi-Strauss (I had no one with whom to discuss this affinity), I wrote a paper on the topic. Without much reflection and with little hope of hearing back, I sent the paper (in English, of course) to both men. I was stunned to receive reflective responses from both of them, both sent on the same day, April 10, 1970! Characteristically, Piaget was entirely positive, while Lévi-Strauss was more critical—and more useful. Those letters are proudly hung in my office, a few feet away from Groucho's witty declination (see the photographs in the first group of photos).

The notice from two outstanding world-class scholars meant a great deal to me. (I don't think any of my classmates or professors in experimental developmental psychology would have cared—we inhabited different universes.) But the thought of linking these two figures did have appeal in the world of publishing. The following year, I signed a contract to publish *The Quest for Mind: Piaget, Lévi-Strauss and the Structuralist Movement*, with Alfred A. Knopf, then, as now, the most prestigious publishing house in the country.

As with *Man and Men* I was able to write quickly, and I completed a book manuscript for *Quest* at about the same time as I completed *The Arts and Human Development*. Unlike *Man and Men*, *Quest* was not a textbook. Unlike *The Arts*, it was not an attempt, probably premature, at an original and perhaps even creative scholarly synthesis. Rather, it was a readable account of the intellectual contributions of two outstanding living scholars; a perhaps original attempt to discern similarities and differences in their work; and, more than either of the other books, an attempt at popularization, a primer for the general educated reader. In this endeavor, I was aided a good deal by Daniel Okrent, the acquiring editor—at that time, barely twenty years old, since then a distinguished editor, author, and the initial ombudsman for the *New York Times*—and Melvin Rosenthal, the best copy editor I've ever had . . . perhaps the best copy editor *anyone* has ever had.

With the benefit of hindsight, I now can see that I was writing three different kinds of books, calling on what I might now term three different kinds of mental operations. In *Man and Men*, I was doing a standard *summary* of the field, as I had learned about it in a single course with some collateral reading over recent years. I was being disciplined and describing a standard subdiscipline.

In *The Arts and Human Development*, I was trying to create a new field of knowledge, or at least a new stance on human development. This was clearly an attempt at a creative leap; and, at its best, it proved useful to myself and to my emerging group of students and colleagues who were also interested in developing a new field of knowledge. But it was probably too academic, and it lacked the empirical basis on which others could readily add their bricks to the building. That was to come in the ensuing years; the conversation would change but not primarily because of my efforts. Indeed, two books by my wife, Ellen Winner, *Invented Worlds* (1982) and *How Art Works* (2018), are the best introductions to this line of work.

In *The Quest for Mind*, I was attempting an original synthesis: putting together the ideas and methods of two outstanding scholars in ways they had not been hitherto combined and thereby helping people to see the two individuals, and their relationships, in ways that had not heretofore been appreciated. And importantly, I was writing for a general public, not for students of social psychology (as in *Man and Men*) or for scholars in aesthetics or in developmental psychology (as in *The Arts and Human Development*).

Yet from the point of view of the writing itself, the process was not very different, and remains pretty much the same to this day, indeed to this hour. I take lots of notes, organize and reorganize them repeatedly, speak to colleagues and friends incessantly about what I have been thinking. And I have constant conversations with myself in my own mind, often creating sentences that could be, and sometimes are, dictated—decades ago into a tape recorder, nowadays into my cell phone.

And then I sit down and write . . . and write, and write. I am not one of those writers who obsesses about the first sentence, or who allots himself five hundred words a day, or who revises the first chapter until it is perfect before moving on. No, I just spit it out (or, if you prefer, crank it out). At least a chapter at a time, and, as far as possible, the whole book in one fell swoop—more precisely, in an uninterrupted week or two of several hours a day at the keyboard. I need to—I want to—get a feeling for the whole enterprise, what the whole book will feel like, even what it will look like in so many words.

In this endeavor I like to think of myself as a composer of a symphony-in-words, who starts by drafting all four (or five or dozen) movements and then fills in the details and edits as necessary, including reconfiguring the main theme or revising the order of sections or chapters.

Once a draft is done, I put it aside for a while and then redo, and redo, and redo. Most of my books go through at least four drafts, and several have gone through more. Often, I will show drafts to friends or colleagues and get their reactions, which I sometimes heed, especially when a particular bit of advice comes from more than one person (though sometimes I stubbornly stick to my guns—sometimes to my ultimate regret). And of course, at a certain point, the manuscript is seen by an editor and then an additional round of writing and rewriting often ensues. Claude Lévi-Strauss said that there are only three happy moments for a book writer: when the book is conceived, when it is ready to be sent out for publication, and when the published book arrives in the mail.

I disagree; I like writing books and hope ardently that I can continue to do so.

So there I was, a young writer of three quite different kinds of books, starting a new area of research in artistic development, soon to be the codirector of Project Zero, happily married to fellow doctoral student Judy, and the father of a growing family (Kerith born in 1969, Jay 1971, Andrew 1976). Perhaps to the outside world, my future vocation and my future kinds of research and writing were evident—but to me, they were shrouded in mystery.

ASSEMBLING A NETWORK OF ENTERPRISES

At age twenty-seven, and in the same ceremony as my wife Judy, I received my doctorate in developmental psychology, technically in social psychology. My formal studies were complete.

But were they? When I had finished college, I had considered a career as a clinical psychologist, but my heart was not really in it. There was only one Erik Erikson; and at any rate I was more attracted to his facility at discerning the telling detail and to his impressive synthesizing capacity than to his notable therapeutic approaches and achievements, mostly with young patients. The subsequent year abroad had been important in consolidating what I had learned in and around college and in providing opportunity to ponder rmore palatable educational and career options. I had some-how gotten through graduate school—initially with stress, later, with more equilibrium. Once again, I realized that I wanted to con-tinue my studies. And with considerable luck, I was able to do so.

Even in that distant era, students receiving a doctoral degree sought postdoctoral fellowships. (Today, this is far more common, though more difficult to accomplish.) Such bonanzas are a way of continuing one's education, pursuing new topics, and at least for a while, avoiding the job market, the daily grind of teaching, and the lifelong routine entailed in having a "real job." Ultimately I applied for and was fortunate to receive three postdoctoral fellowships. I was able to stagger them, so that I had not one or two but three full years in which to continue graduate school, so to speak—and in a way that was happily more reminiscent of the scintillating college years rather than of the Sisyphean graduate school grind. As a bonus, I was also able to put the finishing touches on *The Arts and Human Development* and *The Quest for Mind*.

What to learn, if I were fortunate enough to achieve the gift of one or more additional years? I thought initially of studying art history or aesthetics—tipping toward the humanities. But then I had another one of those unanticipated transformative experiences that directed my curiosity in a new direction.

In the late 1960s, Nelson Goodman, head of Project Zero (PZ), and I learned about exciting new work in brain studies. To counter intractable epilepsy, surgeons had on rare occasions cut the corpus callosum, the band of tissue that joins the two halves of the brain; by virtue of this dramatic surgical intervention, they had effectively separated the left and right hemispheres. Via visual tachistoscopic and dichotic listening techniques (the kind of technologies that I was not skilled at implementing), it became possible to study separately and reliably the capacities of the two halves of the brain—massive tissues that appear to be essentially identical to the naked eye but turn out to facilitate quite different functions. And it turned out that the apparently discrete functions that had been discovered intrigued both Goodman and me.

Fortuitously, one of the leading researchers in this field, neurologist Norman Geschwind, lived and worked nearby, with posts at the Boston Veterans Administration (VA) Hospital and the Harvard Medical School. In those days, as I had learned when inviting famous speakers to speak at Quincy House, it was easier to persuade busy individuals to spend time, without compensation, with students and colleagues at another site. (Nowadays, and I am not being precious or catty, one is fortunate if one receives a polite "no.") Accordingly, Professor Norman Geschwind came over to Cambridge, to the cramped offices of PZ, then on Prescott Street, and spoke to our small yet hearty and dogged group of researchers.

In honesty I can't remember exactly what Geschwind said during the standard two-hour seminar—perhaps because I heard him speak over a hundred times in the subsequent decade and a half, so that the so-called primacy effect was neutralized. I do know that we were all fascinated, indeed mesmerized. So much so that Geschwind stayed over dinner, and while I went home for a while to be with my family, I returned to Project Zero to find the gathering still going strong.

I realized immediately that the work that Geschwind and colleagues were carrying out was highly relevant to issues that, for various reasons, fascinated both Goodman and me. In Goodman's case, he had hypothesized the existence of two kinds of symbol systems: notational symbol systems, which are highly digital—yes/no, on/off—and *non*notational symbols, which are distinctly analog, proceeding in infinite tiny gradations—from orange to red, or from the sound of OH to the sound of AH. Linguistic and musical scores were notational, each symbol denoting a specific referent, while visual arts, such as painting and sculpture, were distinctly nonnotational. You could not reliably designate specific parts of such visual configurations and legislate how they worked together. Interestingly, dance at first appears to be nonnotational, but it proves possible to create quite comprehensive dance notational systems that capture the important features of a specific dance accurately enough that it can be faithfully reproduced in subsequent performances of that dance.

Occasionally nature cooperates with human intuition. Lo and behold, the left hemisphere of the brain seemed to have evolved to process notational/digital symbol systems; while for its part, the right hemisphere of the brain seemed to have evolved to process nonnotational, analog symbol systems. To our astonishment, the brain appeared to honor philosophical distinctions—or perhaps vice versa.

My interest in Geschwind's neurological and neuropsychological investigations took a somewhat different tack. At the time deeply involved in trying to understand how artistic skills and talents develop, I had found it difficult to disentangle various capacities from one another. To take one example: Do music and language involve the same abilities and skills, being roughly similar to one another, like two eyes or two ears? Or are they quite separate from one another, like, say, the kidney and the stomach? Or to consider yet another possibility, does one human faculty piggyback on the other, with language growing out of music, or vice versa?

With ordinary individuals, lay or expert, it is not readily possible to disentangle language from music. But brain injury can change that state of affairs abruptly and dramatically. The brain can be damaged via stroke (tissue disabled in either hemisphere, on the surface or in the deeper regions of the cortex), via trauma (a bullet, a missile), or via disease (a slow- or fast-growing tumor). And when an individual suffers damage to the brain, it becomes possible to discern the relation—or alternatively, the *lack* of relation—between two mental faculties. As Geschwind explained: when composer Maurice Ravel became aphasic, he was still able to appreciate and critique musical performances; and when painter Lovis Corinth suffered damage to the right hemisphere, he could still draw, but he eliminated or distorted information on the left side of the canvas.

With dramatic swiftness and finality, my riddle of *what* subject to pursue should I receive a postdoctoral fellowship was resolved. Shortly after the PZ talk, I asked Professor Geschwind whether he would agree to be my sponsor for a postdoctoral application. And even though I was not a physician and he was already a distinguished and much-sought-after mentor, he kindly agreed to do so. I remember vividly—more vividly than I remember the details of his hours-long stint at Project Zero—that I arranged to sit near him on a flight to Miami, where he was to give a keynote address at a psychology conference that I was attending. Moving to the adjoining seat in economy class, I dared to show him my application for a postdoctoral fellowship. Professor Geschwind leafed through it, at a speed that most of us reserve for perusing magazines stacked in a dental office; pointed out three things that should be changed; and the application was effectively ready for submission.

Of course, at the time there was no guarantee that I would get any fellowship. And so I also applied for one job, an assistant professorship in psychology at Yale University. My formal talk and my conversations with faculty went OK, so far as I could tell, but I was not surprised when I did not get the job. After all, as my efforts to publish in conventional journals had taught me, an interest in artistic development was not seen as a high priority by tenured psychology professors at an Ivy League school, let alone by prestigious editors of prestigious journals or, as irreverent Howie might have put it, editors and journals that *believed themselves* to be prestigious. And they were apparently not impressed by my efforts to carry out standard studies in experimental psychology, nor my efforts to synthesize the work of others in articles and drafts of books. As it happens, the job went to a Stanford graduate David Henry Feldman—soon to become a friend—but he too was becoming interested in "softer" topics (gifted children) and soon found himself leaving Yale for a more secure job in a child studies program at Tufts University.

We all play "it might have been" scenarios or "alternate histories," as they've come to be called. What would have happened if I had gone to Andover rather than to Wyoming Seminary; to Haverford College rather than to Harvard College; to Yale University as a junior professor rather than to the Boston Veterans Administration Hospital as a postdoc? All I can say is: I am glad, relieved that I did *not* get the job at Yale, because the Geschwind/VA link became transformative in so many ways. I remained as a researcher in neuropsychology at the VA for twenty years and it fundamentally and permanently affected how I think about the mind and other matters. I can add that I don't think I would ever have received a tenured professorship in a standard psychology department. I am too much of a maverick, odd ball, or eccentric.

In retrospect, I can identify one of the reasons why the work with Geschwind and the brain proved so attractive to me. My natural inclinations, dating back to high school if not to second grade, were to read, observe, chatter, synthesize, write, and rewrite. That is what I had done in the *Opinator*, the senior seminar, my Harvard College classes, and my disparate pursuits in graduate school. As had been the case with economist John Kenneth Galbraith, the normal English language allowed me to say what I wanted to say in the way that I wanted to say it—synthesizing psychological and sociological perspectives, as one might characterize it in an academic context.

And yet, it is now clear to me that I was also looking for *dry land*, for a more formal and defensible basis on which to base my claims and my conclusions. I loved the straightforward descriptions of children in Piaget's workaday prose, and the portrayals of other cultures in the far more evocative writings of Claude Lévi-Strauss. But I was also attracted to the introduction of logical formulas: the algebraic structures and mechanisms that are hypothesized to underlie human behavior.

In Piaget's case, he drew on formal logic, which he then adopted in ways that irritated most logicians, to explain the less rigorous but still formalizable reasoning that putatively underlies children's words and actions. In Lévi-Strauss's case he invoked logical schemas, particularly ones borrowed from the study of linguistic phonology, but also from other mathematical and notational systems. Specifically, Lévi-Strauss adopted and adapted these lenses to explicate the sources and organization of kinship structures, residential patterns, and, most evocatively, the characters and actions and natural phenomena that recur in scores of myths from tribal societies scattered across the globe.

To this day I am not sure whether I was personally enchanted by these formalisms or whether I was drawn to them because they placed my own musings and conclusions on firmer ground.

Nowadays, I am skeptical that such algebraic formalisms added much to the contributions of two great scholars. Piaget's and Lévi-Strauss's methods were certainly very Cartesian, very French, but perhaps also very pretentious. Still, for whatever reason, I continued to search for such firm underpinnings. To retrieve a recollection from a different context: after a heated discussion, Jerry Bruner once asked me if I had majored in physics! Nothing had been further from my mind, or indeed my capacities; but it flattered me to think that I could ever come off as a student of the physical, as opposed to the biological or social, sciences.

The chain of reasoning is clear: If you are studying the mind, what could be a *firmer terra* than the brain? Only a mystic would locate cognitive and other psychological capacities outside of the nervous system. And so, if one studied the brain carefully, and also observed directly and firsthand what happens when the brain is damaged, then one's conclusions about the organization of human performances could be much more convincing, and indeed much more conclusive.

Still, this line of reasoning can be deceptive. We now know that many persons will place much more faith in a scientific article if it features a few photographs of the brain, even if the contents of the article are *identical* to one devoid of such illustration. Moreover, to jump ahead a little, I don't think that as educators we should *ever* do anything differently *just because* of newly acquired information about the operations of the brain.

Nonetheless, so long as one bears those cautions in mind, it is certainly valuable, perhaps invaluable, to know about the structure and functioning of the brain. Even though I have long since forgotten them, I don't regret the many hours I spent mastering various lobes and fissures depicted in the Sidman & Sidman illustrated catalog of brain structures and connections. And I looked forward eagerly to the medical rounds, particularly when they were led by Norman Geschwind. On those weekly rounds at the VA, all the practitioners on the aphasia (or neurology) ward would meet a patient; hear him (as veterans, the patients were at this time almost always men) being interviewed by a clinician; listen to the reports from various specialists such as speech pathologists, psychologists, linguists; and then all of us would hazard a guess on where the brain lesion or damage was likely to be located and with what size, shape, and disrupted connections. After everyone, including Geschwind, had placed a bet (so to speak), the neuroradiologist would unveil the brain scan or CT scan—the measures of the time that now seem so primitive. In the succeeding moments of discussion and debate, the assembled clinicians and researchers would add to our knowledge of brain structures and functions as they relate to concomitant psychological performances. In short: a scientific guessing game followed by discussion and, at least in some cases, illumination.

At any rate, the applications for support came through: and ultimately three years of postdoctoral fellowship support transmogrified into a twenty-year routine. In the mornings, I would travel to the Boston Veterans Administration Hospital (now a Medical Center) and spend several hours observing and carrying out various kinds of experimental studies with individuals who had suffered brain damage—damage that was ultimately verified and quantified by the neuroanatomical, neurophysiological and, neuroelectronic measures of the day.

In the afternoons, I would drive from the bowels of Boston to the relative greenery of Cambridge (searching, all too often in vain, for a convenient parking space) and hang my hat at Project Zero—still alive, sometimes thriving. Once I became codirector, in 1972, I had administrative tasks to carry out. But the principal reason for remaining with PZ was the opportunity to carry out research in cognitive development, exceedingly broadly construed to incorporate the range of artistic forms, with children of different ages. Often the research would occur in schools, and I, with a growing team of talented colleagues, would spend time in nearby Belmont or Brookline or Arlington or Newton "testing rooms" with young people ranging in age from pre-kindergarteners to high schoolers.

What issues were my research team and I pursuing in these two venues, with these two quite different populations: the schools, representing aspirations for the future, and the neurology wards, containing a population with less sanguine prospects?[1]

I can now answer that question quite crisply. We were trying to do for the arts what Jean Piaget, Jerome Bruner, and other developmentalists had been pursuing with respect to logical and scientific thinking. With children, we were studying the *development of the skills and understandings that are needed to be a successful participant in the arts*. With brain-damaged patients, à la Geschwind and his colleagues, we were studying the ways in which *competences important in the arts break down, or are spared*, in the wake of one or another form and site of brain damage. And of course, as an inveterate reader and synthesizer of "the literature," I was continuously trying

---

1. It's worth mentioning that my colleagues and I at the VA Hospital devised two therapies that had some effectiveness, with the intriguing names of "Melodic Intonation Therapy" or MIT and "Visual Communication Therapy" or VIC.

to put these parts of the puzzle together to build a model of artistic competence: its components, their integration into smoothly functioning artistry, and, less happily, their dissolution under various forms of damage to the brain. Although neither the children not the veterans were artists like Maurice Ravel or Lovis Corinth, the studies we undertook attempted to figure out the basic components of artistry and then probe their development and their breakdown.

Consider a sample area already mentioned in the previous chapter: the creation and understanding of metaphor, a key aspect of linguistic arts in poems, stories, novels, and plays. I asked subjects to explain the meaning of a metaphor, or, particularly apt with patients who were aphasic, to match a phrase to an appropriate illustration. In the case of children, after an early period of metaphoric flowering in speech, children become very literal minded. And so, if you talk about someone's heart hardening, these literally minded youngsters are likely to choose an illustration where someone has a heart that appears to be made of stone. Our team dubbed this stage of development the "literal stage," and it's a stage that at least some adults never outgrow.

What of brain-damaged patients? Well, here's the obvious prediction. When patients become aphasic, as typically happens following damage to the left hemisphere of the brain, they should be unable to appreciate metaphor; in cases where they sustain damage to the right hemisphere of the brain, which spares language, they should remain OK.

But in fact, the results of our investigations were counterintuitive. Despite their aphasia, most aphasic patients would choose the correct illustration, say, of a person looking despondent. Indeed, such patients would sometimes laugh out loud at the illustration of the person lugging around a heart made of stone. In contrast, the patients with right hemisphere disease, despite their supposedly intact language faculties, would often choose the depiction of the person with the stone heart. They resembled children at the literal stage of development.

This finding had profound implications for our understanding of language and the brain. Syntax, phonology, and literal semantics appear to be housed in the left hemisphere (in right-handed persons) and are therefore impaired by brain damage to that half of the nervous system. But the ability to "go beyond the literal"—to get at connotation as well as denotation—seems to be a property of the right, or so-called nonlinguistic hemisphere and is therefore impaired by brain damage. Sensitivity to evocative speech acts such as metaphor, sarcasm, irony is diminished in cases of patients who sustain right-hemisphere damage.

Of course, all researchers are putting together tiny pieces of a giant puzzle, as the metaphor goes (excuse me!), placing an additional brick in the massive and often mysterious edifice of science. And that is what Ellen Winner, Hiram Brownell, and I did in our research on literal and nonliteral language. I've studied numerous psychological processes with both children and brain-damaged patients, and colleagues and I have published well over one hundred peer-reviewed articles. But I think that the work on nonliteral language and the brain is the most important, and perhaps the *only* important, contribution that I've made to experimental science. And I'm pleased that over the years, many researchers, including Ellen and Hiram, have carried out descendants or offspring of this work, if you'll pardon the predictable metaphor.

Yes, I could raise money for observational and experimental studies, carry out research (typically with the simplest possible technologies), write them up, and even get them published in appropriate
journals. Rather than adding to the file of unpublished work that
my teacher Roger Brown had warned me about, almost every study
that my colleagues and I did—with children, with brain-damaged
patients, and with both populations—found an appropriate journal.[2]

But even at that now distant time, it was becoming clear to me
that many people could design and carry out empirical psychological studies as well as I could, and there were many more young
researchers who were technologically or technically far more skilled
than I could ever hope to become. I sometimes quip that, with exqui-
site timing, I left the field of neuropsychology at the very time that far
more sophisticated measures of neural activity like MRIs and PET
scans were becoming widely available to resourceful researchers.

My competitive advantage lay elsewhere. I was curious; I could
read rapidly and widely; I enjoyed synthesizing and resynthesizing.
I could also write quickly and clearly; and I could address various
audiences, including the intelligent general reader. And so, while
continuing for decades to contribute modestly to the peer-reviewed
empirical literature, and training my students in that science and
art, I became more of a writer, and strove (with limited but not
negligible success) to be a public intellectual—a "poor man's" psy-
chologically trained aspirant to the mantles of my one-time heroes
Edmund Wilson and Richard Hofstadter.

---

2. It was easier to get published in those days; and I was quite resourceful
in finding publishing outlets on those occasions where the leading journals
rejected the research reports.

During the 1970s I became a columnist for *Psychology Today* (which was, if I may be permitted a self-serving phrase, a far more serious publication in those days); I wrote regularly for the *New York Times*, both occasional pieces and book reviews; I contributed as well to other newspapers and periodicals; and I began to appear in the media, especially on public radio and, at a time when those broadcasting outlets were much more open to academics, the morning television talk shows. My experience on the radio musical program junior judges, two decades earlier, had not been entirely in vain.

I also continued to write books. My experience with brain-damaged patients convinced me that, in the days before the writings of neurologist Oliver Sacks rose to deserved prominence, the world of aphasia, alexia, agnosia, and other cortical disorders constituted a terrain virtually unknown to the general public. Accordingly, I wrote a second book for the publisher Alfred A. Knopf, *The Shattered Mind: The Person after Brain Damage*. Having children who were budding artists (and who are still artistically inclined, and far more "visual" than their dad), I studied their output as well as that of other children; and, having been prodded thereafter by my editor at Knopf to find another, more research-oriented publisher, I placed *Artful Scribbles: The Significance of Children's Drawings* with Basic Books. I put most of my columns for *Psychology Today* together in a collection of essays, appropriately entitled *Art, Mind, and Brain*, also published by Basic Books.

Probably most notably, I wrote a textbook called *Developmental Psychology*, which was originally considered eccentric by the authors of the then best-selling text in the area, but which nonetheless sold very well. As mentioned before, I might have had a successful, even lucrative, life as a textbook writer. I was becoming a skilled summarizer and synthesizer of the works of other scholars. But, intellectually restless, I was very relieved ultimately not to have to continue down that path.

While I was writing for various outlets, and carrying out research with children and brain-damaged patients, Project Zero continued to grow. Codirector Dave Perkins and I soon catalyzed several different lines of research both within and beyond artistic cognition. To borrow a phrase of the realm, we were presiding over "an expanding network of enterprise." It turns out that introverted Howie, who had lived for decades largely in his mind, was a reasonably good manager and a reasonably skilled fundraiser. (Though we complemented one another, the same descriptors could be applied to Dave.) I was also fortunate to belong to a couple of "invisible colleges." These groups of scholars managed to get together opportunistically at professional conferences and other gatherings to discuss issues of common interest that were not yet discernible on the broader academic radar screen.

One such was a group of psychologists, linguists, communication experts, and art experts who were interested in the nature and operations of different symbol systems, à la Nelson Goodman. Fittingly, we called ourselves "the symbol system group." Another invisible college was composed of scholars, most quite senior to me, who brought a social scientific lens to the arts. This group included psychologist Rudolf Arnheim, visual arts educator Elliot Eisner, and music educator Bennett Reimer. I also joined and became active in two groups of neuropsychological researchers: a US-based one called the Academy of Aphasia, and a largely European one called, appropriately, the International Neuropsychology Symposium. Since at the time I did not belong to an academic department with concomitant faculty colleagues, these became my collegial homes. So even though I was not teaching regularly, and therefore, unlike almost all of my peers and colleagues, was continuing to live on "soft money," I managed to survive and even to thrive, while supporting a growing family.

Of course, not every endeavor in this emerging set of enterprises was successful. One disappointment was a major research project on the development of symbolic competence in young children, which sadly was never completed. But as I was to learn from my subsequent study of the great economist and Europeanist Jean Monnet, "one should regard every defeat as an opportunity." And paradoxically, the failure of the ambitious "early symbolization project" may well have catalyzed the devising of the work for which I am best known: the theory of multiple intelligences.

Howard's grandfather, Martin Weilheimer.

Howard and his sister, Marion, around 1954.

Howard's uncle, Fred Gardner, and father, Ralph Gardner.

Future Student of Leadership

Howard photographing Adlai Stevenson, Democratic candidate for president,
in 1956.

Howard at his confirmation, 1959.

GROUCHO MARX
1083 Hillcrest Road
Beverly Hills, California

October 16, 1968

Mr. Howard Gardner
Quincy House #8
Harvard University
Cambridge 38, Massachusetts

Dear Mr. Gardner:

I'm flattered that you want me to speak to the
inmates of Quincy House, however, I am still
working - it's called "making a living". Kind
of an old fashioned phrase, but it keeps your
family from starving. Anyway, what little energy
I have left is directed toward performing in various shows and when I do have to travel East for
one of these performances, I hustle back home to
the hills of Beverly just as soon as I'm finished.

What I'm trying to say is, thanks a lot for asking
me but I'll have to pass.

Regards,

Groucho

GM:jn

Letter from Groucho Marx.

Genève, le 1o avril 197o

Monsieur Howard GARDNER
Harvard University
Department of Social Relations
William James Hall 1257
CAMBRIDGE , Mass. o2138

Cher Docteur Gardner,

J'ai bien reçu et j'ai lu avec grand plaisir vos deux belles études sur Levi Strauss et sur moi. Elles sont remarquables de finesse et de pénétration et je vous en félicite. C'est un plaisir de lire des gens qui vous comprennent et cela n'arrive pas tous les jours.

J'aimerais seulement vous signaler à propos de l'article de Parsons sur mon utilisation de la logique formelle, que Parsons m'a très mal compris. Le mathématicien et logicien Seymour Papert, qui enseigne au M.I.T. et que vous connaissez sans doute, avait fait une réponse pour montrer que ma logique était bien sûr différente du calcul des propositions classiques, mais qu'elle était consistante et répondait bien aux besoins psychologiques voulus. Malheureusement le British Journal of Psychology a refusé de publier cette étude de Papert, pour éviter une polémique. J'ai trouvé cela malhonnête, mais surtout regrettable, parce que Papert disait des choses nouvelles et importantes.

D'autre part, le logicien belge Apostel a fait un article dans le même sens, mais qui n'a pas non plus paru. Par contre d'autres logiciens, et en particulier Jean-Blaise Grize, ont décidé de rééditer mon Traité de logiqu en fournissant aux lecteurs des informations suffisantes pour qu'ils comprennent les points de vue nouveaux qu'il contient. Je vous signale tout cela pour que vous puissiez renseigner éventuellement vos lecteurs sur ces points où il y a eu malentendu complet avec les logiciens.

En vous remerciant encore très vivement, je vous prie, cher Docteur Gardner, de croire à mes sentiments les meilleurs.

J. PIAGET

Letter from Jean Piaget.

LABORATOIRE D'ANTHROPOLOGIE SOCIALE

DU COLLÈGE DE FRANCE ET DE L'ÉCOLE PRATIQUE DES HAUTES ÉTUDES

TÉL. 633-79-10 OU
033-61-60 ET 326-26-63 (POSTE 211)

11 PLACE MARCELIN-BERTHELOT
PARIS 5

Paris, April 10, 1970

Dr. Howard Gardner
Harvard University
Department of Social Relations
William James Hall 1257
Cambridge, Massachusetts 02138
U.S.A.

Dear Mr. Gardner,

Many thanks for sending me your two papers which I read with great interest. I fully agree with the parallel you draw between Piaget and I, except that it seems to me that you have overlooked two points. In the first place, Piaget is substantially older than I am and since he started publishing very early he was already read and lectured upon when I was still a student at the University. In the second place, there are in fact two Piagets, the early one with whom I am not in great sympathy and the later one whom, on the contrary, I admire greatly

Concerning your other paper, to be quite frank, the kind of criticism you level at me makes me shrug. I look at myself as a rustic explorer equipped with a woodman's axe to open a path in an unknown land and you reproach me for not having yet drawn a complete map, calculated accurate my bearings and for not having yet landscaped the country ! Forgive me f saying so but it looks as if Lewis and Clark were taken to task for not having designed the plans of General Motors while on their way to Oregon Science is not the work of one man. I may have broken new ground but it will take a great many years and the labour of many individuals to till and make the harvest.

With best regards.

Sincerely yours,

Claude Lévi-Strauss

CLS:eg

Letter from Claude Lévi-Strauss.

Nelson Goodman.

Norman Geschwind (right) and Howard at a party.

Jerome Bruner, on his ninety-fifth birthday, with Howard.

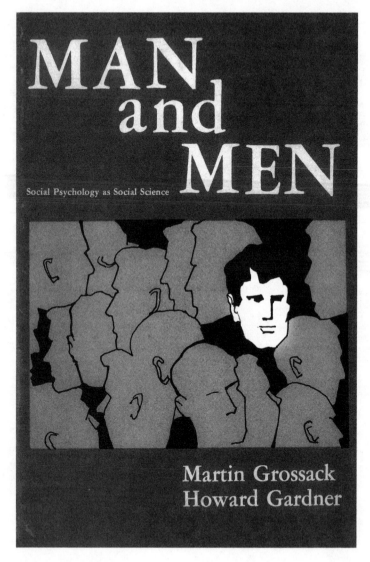

MAN
and
MEN

Social Psychology as Social Science

Martin Grossack
Howard Gardner

Cover of *Man and Men*.

II

MULTIPLE INTELLIGENCES: REFRAMING A HUMAN CONVERSATION

STEPS TOWARD *FRAMES*

Early in 1979, Paul Ylvisaker, then the dean of the Harvard Graduate School of Education, called me into his office. A former state
administrator of New Jersey and grants officer at the Ford Foundation, Ylvisaker wanted to discuss a big idea. He sat on the board of
the Bernard van Leer Foundation, a Dutch philanthropy that was
little known in the United States. For his own reasons, Oscar van
Leer, the sometimes errant and often grandiose son of entrepreneur
Bernard, was commissioning a study of "the nature and realization
of human potential." Dean Ylvisaker asked if I and colleague Harry
Lasker would like to head such a study.

I had not heard of the foundation, I did not know Harry Lasker
well, and my relations with the dean had been, at best, polite and
distant. Indeed, in 1972 at the start of what turned out to be a rocky
decanal regime, Dean Ylvisaker had tried to get rid of Project Zero,
the organization where I had carried out my research and through

which I had maintained a connection to Harvard—essential for fund-raising purposes. Project Zero was spared the chopping block only thanks to the interventions of the dean's own sister, Barbara Y. Newsome, who worked for a prestigious New York foundation, and of Israel Scheffler, a well-regarded senior professor at Harvard who decades before had been Nelson Goodman's student and then colleague. With Project Zero over half a century old today, and my professional life intertwined forever with that curiously dubbed organization, I owe both Barbara and Is a tremendous debt and a measure of gratitude as well to Dean Ylvisaker.

Nonetheless, to tweak a phrase borrowed from my own mentor Erik Erikson, I was "a young scholar with some talent but no place to go"—not a professor at Harvard, not a medical researcher at the VA, not a recognized public intellectual—and I certainly did not want to be identified and remembered chiefly as a writer of psychology textbooks. And so, with little hesitation, I accepted the assignment and opportunity proffered by the dean. For the next five years I was a principal investigator and a leader of the Harvard Project on Human Potential (PHP). As it turned out, the PHP gave me the resources and the latitude, eventually, to create and write about the theory of multiple intelligences.

Shortly after assuming this role, I made a decision. As a key researcher on the project, I assigned myself the task of *synthesizing all that was known* about human cognitive potentials. Having already written two books with the word "mind" in the title—*The Quest for Mind* and *The Shattered Mind*—and about to publish a third—*Art, Mind, and Brain*—it seemed appropriate for me to survey the potentials of the human mind. And this generously funded study gave me the opportunity to build on two of my own investigative platforms that had, for various reasons, not reached completion.

Shortly after completing *The Shattered Mind* (published in 1975), I had outlined a book called *Kinds of Minds*. Having for several years studied concurrently the development *and* the breakdown of mind, I was reflecting on whether members of the human species foreground a range of minds, just as we foreground a range of senses, personalities, and ambitions. This book plan was put aside and indeed forgotten (or perhaps repressed?) until a few years ago, when I discovered the aforementioned outline in a box of ancient papers. Just as my teacher Roger Brown had consoled me by saying that he and colleagues had files of unpublished research papers, I think that I speak for most aspiring authors of books in saying that we have boxes of notes compiled for books that were never completed and may even have been erased from recall.

The second project was the ambitious study of the development of symbol-using capacities in children that I had embarked on a few years earlier with a young colleague, Dennie Wolf. This study was deliberately patterned after Jean Piaget's pioneering studies of his own three children. Carrying out simple but clever bedside experiments over the years with young Laurent, Lucienne, and Jacqueline, Piaget had traced the origins and developments of the so-called Kantian categories: how children acquire an initial sense of *time, space, number, causality*, and other basic mental structures, into which, according to Immanuel Kant, all experience is necessarily apprehended, processed, manipulated, and perhaps transformed. To cite one well-known example, Piaget showed that until the latter part of the first year of life, infants persist in searching for an object where it was first seen, rather than shifting their search to the locus to which it had been transported in front of their own eyes.

We elected to study nine children in the Boston area—a small sample, but three times as large as Piaget's own "data base." Through weekly observations and many informal tests and measures, we and our research colleagues examined the development of language (specifically, figurative language and storytelling); musical expression; two-dimensional depiction (drawing); three-dimensional expression (clay construction, block building); and bodily expression (dance). Note that each of these capacities had an artistic flavor, which reflected the research focus of Project Zero in its early years. Anyone familiar with the argument of "multiple intelligences" or "MI theory" (yet to emerge in my own mind and yet to be described in this memoir) will also recognize the kinship of these symbol-using capacities with the list of intelligences that I ultimately put forth, although the differences turn out to be equally revealing. We also examined the development of numerical sophistication, as a kind of a "control" symbol system. This form of symbol use, central to the scientific mind although much less relevant to most artistry, linked our work more directly to that of Piaget and other mainstream developmental psychologists.

For a while Dennie and I worked well together. We analyzed much of the incoming data and published some papers on early findings. An intriguing contrast among the children concerned their approach to play. Some of the nine children we termed "patterners." Given objects to play with, they did not say a lot, but they put together interesting and often quite complex spatial arrays. Others we termed "dramatists." These youngsters, far more talkative, were prone to storytelling and to pretend or dramatic play.

But alas, as almost any lifelong researcher will acknowledge, not all research plans pan out. Difficulties arose over whose data these were, how to analyze them, how to write them up, and probably most important, what overall story we should tell and in what form and via what format. There is no point, decades later, in assigning any blame. I finally relinquished the materials of the project to Dennie. Though the subjects of the study are now in their forties, the work has never been properly published, and Piaget's scheme of cognitive development remains without a serious counter-story or complementary story. The inglorious demise of the early symbolization project is perhaps my greatest regret as an empirical researcher.

At any rate, with "kinds of minds" and "the early symbolization project" in the back of my mind, and with a generous, multiyear budget from the Van Leer foundation, I put together a small research team. We began our search for the nature and realization of human potential, with "human cognition writ large" as our major focus.

What turned out to be a large, perhaps even massive, undertaking allowed me to go well beyond my earlier thinking and empirical research in at least three ways:

I was clearly reaching beyond the arts—an admittedly important but still limited form of cognition—and attempting to survey the full gamut of human thought.

I was going beyond my subdiscipline of developmental psychology to the full spectrum of psychology, and to a wide span of other disciplines, ranging from anthropology to genetics. An expanded and updated version of Soc Rel, one might say.

I had the unanticipated and invaluable opportunity to examine these issues beyond the shores of the United States.

Around that time, I had spoken to H. Thomas (Tom) James, president of the Spencer Foundation, a formidable Chicago-based philanthropy that had been supporting our work ever since I had received my doctorate. The remit of the foundation was to support research in education, but at that time much of the funding went to broader social scientific and biological research, including those lines of research undertaken by select members of the invisible colleges to which I belonged. Having codirected Project Zero for some time, and being unsure about where next to take it, I posed the quandary to Tom James. With barely a second's hesitation Tom said, "Take it international . . . or give it a decent burial." I chose the former course and Project Zero eventually made the same choice.

Five years of funding (which eventually became six) from the Van Leer Foundation gave my colleagues and me the chance to "take it international." Not only did we read widely about the varieties of human potential discerned and promoted in diverse historical and cross-cultural sources; we also had the chance to bring in colleagues from around the world and to travel alone, or as a group, far and wide. I had been to Europe several times but not elsewhere. On the Van Leer project, courtesy of its generous budget, I not only visited many research sites in Europe, making at least half a dozen trips to the foundation headquarters in the Hague, but also traveled widely in Asia (China, Japan, Hong Kong, the latter then a separate crown colony), Latin America (Mexico), and North Africa (Egypt, Senegal, the Gambia), as well as attending international gatherings in various places.

I have noted that, more than most individuals, I live inside my head. That said, I confirmed first hand that there is no substitute for spending time in other countries and cultures; getting to know from two to five researchers, helped me to dig deeper into many sources of information. We surveyed not only studies of the brain but also research on genetics, including the fascinating documentation of which traits are heritable and to what degree and under what circumstances. We surveyed the findings emanating from psychometric measures: intelligence testing but also the testing of personality, motivation, emotion, and character. We surveyed findings in anthropology, including studies of abilities, behaviors, work, and leisure pursuits across a wide range of cultures all over the globe, including ones that were essentially preliterate (the Puluwat sailors of the Caroline Islands in the South Seas), as well as ones that were more ancient and arguably more sophisticated than Western ones (China). We looked at the history and the prehistory of human aspirations: faith in progress and possibility; cyclical views; belief in incarnation and reincarnation; as well as more dystopic views, starting with the Fall from Paradise. We even carried out philosophical analyses of the notions of progress, potential, and human nature.

As someone whose scholarly forte has been reading, questioning, discussing, synthesizing, and writing, this was a dream assignment. I met and talked with my research team at least weekly and sometimes daily. I enjoyed regular discussions with senior colleagues at the Harvard Graduate School of Education—social psychologist Gerald Lesser, anthropologist Robert LeVine, philosopher Israel Scheffler, and sociologist Merry "Corky" White—and from around the globe, as well as with colleague Harry Lasker. But in the end, and particularly at the end, this was largely a solitary undertaking.

At home, on weekends, on long trips, I sat with paper and pencil (no computers yet!) and created various taxonomies. Some taxonomies had to do with various modes and means of scholarly analysis drawn from the relevant disciplines; some taxonomies had to do with various observations and descriptions of roles, occupations, forms of expertise; some taxonomies had to do with specific lists of human capacities and talents; some surveyed different regions of the brain or of the planet. Neither I nor anyone else would want to have to review (or re-view) all of those jottings. People listened politely to what I had to say and sometimes read and critiqued my charts and my drafts, but it was my thing—my quixotic quest, so to speak.

Ultimately, I came up with a dozen or so possible human cognitive capacities, some drawn from our own research, some from our reading, some from our discussions and debates. One puzzle was the relation between these capacities and human sensory systems: visual, auditory, tactile. Another puzzle emerged with respect to the size and scope of the territory covered by these capacities. Is language one capacity or a bundle of separate capacities: phonological, syntactic, literary, metaphoric, spoken, written, and so on? Yet another puzzle concerned breadth. Should these capacities be restricted to problem-solving (a psychologist's traditional view of cognition), or should they be much broader, extending to creating, to inventing, to dreaming?

At the same time, I was wrestling with the question of *which* criteria should be applied to determine *whether* a candidate capacity actually qualified for a place on the magical final list to which I was aspiring. Drawing on different disciplines and diverse bodies of knowledge, I ultimately delineated eight criteria:

1. The possibility that a capacity could be isolated (destroyed or spared) by damage to the brain.

2. The existence of specific populations—prodigies, savants—who displayed unusual strength in one capacity, and, often, relative weaknesses in others.

3. An identifiable core operation or set of operations. Here I was drawing explicitly on the model of a computer: could one identify the computations (I used the phrase "basic information-processing operations") that were distinctive to a putative capacity?

4. A distinctive developmental history and a definable set of expert "end state" performances. Here I was leaning on my own training in developmental psychology. For any significant competence, we should be able to lay out an initial condition, a set of steps or stages through which individuals pass as a result of experience, and a vision of the full-blown adult, expert competence. This was unquestionably a Piagetian lens, though one broadened to include artistic and social as well as scientific ways of knowing. And, unlike Piaget, I did not assume that the various capacities emerged at roughly the same time; in any given individual, one form of cognition might well be more or less sophisticated than other hypothesized forms of cognition.

5. An evolutionary history and evolutionary plausibility. Though the field now called "evolutionary psychology" had scarcely been launched, I sought evidence that a candidate capacity met some kind of survival need, and that there were reasons why it had endured and evolved as it had.

6. Support from experimental psychological tasks. Many of the candidate competences had been probed in psychological studies. I was interested in the extent to which one competence correlated or failed to correlate with another. As an example, would the processing of musical information interfere with or foster

the processing of linguistic (or, for that matter, numerical) information? Also, I wondered whether acuteness of memory (or attention or perception) for one kind of information (say, spatial) correlated with acuteness of memory for other kinds of information (say, linguistic or personal). Or, in the same vein, how localized or general are other important capacities, such as attention or perception?

7. Support from psychometric findings. While much of my work would ultimately be critical of standard tests of standard academic competences (typical measures of IQ), I certainly wanted to take into account what we had been established about measures of different capacities and the extent to which they correlate, or fail to correlate, with one another. This criterion has turned out to be the most controversial, since so much of psychological testing indicates that performances purporting to measure various human capacities are correlated with one another. To use the jargon, there is a "positive manifold" across many psychological tests.

8. Susceptibility to encoding in a symbol system. Here the contributions of my philosophical mentor Nelson Goodman and my earlier readings of philosopher Susanne Langer came to the fore. It seemed important that capacities with a raw computational base (criterion 3) and an evolutionary basis (criterion 5) could be captured in a symbol system. This potential for symbolization characterizes capacities that human beings maintain, cherish, embroider, and occasionally transform and pass on to the next generation. As I came to express it, "While it may be possible for an intelligence to proceed without its own special symbol system . . . a primary characteristic of human intelligence may well

be its 'natural' gravitation toward embodiment in a symbolic system" (*Frames of Mind*, 66).

So I had my candidate capacities and I had my criteria. I schematized these in many diagrams along the lines shown in the figure below.

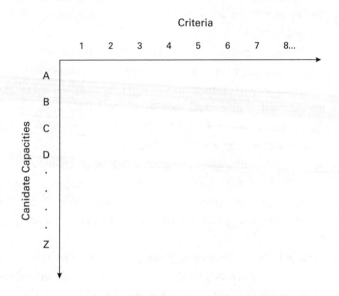

Two tasks remained. First, I needed to whittle down the candidate list to those that most adequately fit the criteria that I had outlined. Then I needed to give appropriate names to the candidate capacities, and ultimately to the ensemble of capacities.

The first task took by far the most time. I ended up with a list of seven competences. They are listed here along with occupational or avocational roles—in both modern and more traditional societies—that draw on that particular competence:

1. Linguistic—think lawyer, poet, journalist, storyteller
2. Logical-mathematical—think scientist, accountant, computer expert, trader, timekeeper

Note: The initial duo encompasses the capacities that are valorized in Western style schools and that are typically measured in intelligence tests. The more an occupation or hobby resembles school—especially a Western school from the last century or so—the more accurately an IQ test score predicts performance in that vocation or avocation.

3. Musical—think composer, singer, instrumentalist, chanter, improviser, devoted fan, or critic
4. Spatial—think large-scale space, like a navigator or pilot; think more local space, like a chess player, mapmaker, or sculptor
5. Bodily kinesthetic (sometimes abbreviated as b-k)—think whole-body competence, as in an athlete or dancer or hunter; or finer-grained competence, as in a weaver or archer, lab technician or surgeon

And finally, two competences that deal with knowledge of human beings:

6. Interpersonal—knowledge of and skill in dealing with other persons; think political leader, salesperson, religious leader, "wise" man or woman, shaman
7. Intrapersonal—think of a person who has a good understanding of him- or herself and can operate cogently on the basis of that understanding. I often quip that only an insightful psychotherapist has the *wherewithal* to judge a particular individual's self-knowledge. But we can all think of persons who introspect

frequently, who learn from experience and who accordingly can anticipate what they will do and how they will feel thereafter. We can as well think of others, in contrast, who, whatever their IQ, seem oblivious to their own reactions and who, as a result, make essentially the same mistake over and over again.

It has probably occurred to you that these latter two capacities are often described as social and emotional capacities; later they got yoked to the noun "intelligence," as in "emotional intelligence" and "social intelligence."

There. I've written the word! Before committing my list to print and revealing or announcing it to the wider world, I had to decide *what to call, what to name* these competences, these kinds of minds. I wish I (or others) could remember the exact circumstances under which I decided—a decision that turned out to be pivotal, fateful, possibly life changing—to call these competences *intelligences*. But I did. And while I sweated for years in identifying potential competences, in laying out the criteria by which to judge them, and in then singling out seven key competences, *it was the pluralization of the single, simple, four-syllable word that turned out in the end to "make all the difference."*

We can't do the experiment, but I am convinced that I would not be writing this memoir, and would not have achieved a certain degree of notoriety if I had chosen some other noun: seven *capacities*; or seven *competences*; or seven *kinds of minds*, recalling the book that I had outlined some years earlier; or seven *talents* or seven *gifts*, or even, to use a phrase I detest, seven *learning styles*. No, with little doubt, it was by virtue of the decision to beg, borrow, seize, or steal the word *intelligence* that I caught the attention of so many readers, including the then all powerful members of the so-called chattering classes.

Ever since Alfred Binet (1857–1911), a great French psychologist, the use of the word "intelligence" and the instrument called the "intelligence quotient test" or the "IQ test" has taken on a special, even sacred meaning in much of the Western world. We want to be intelligent ourselves; we want to know and befriend people who are intelligent; and above all, we want our children to be intelligent.[1]

How best to convey that capacity to the world? Take a short-answer, multiple-choice style test, tote up the right and wrong answers, and compare your performance with that of peers. If you do about as well as others in your cohort, you'll be called *average*. If you do better, say by a standard deviation, you'll be called *smart*; and if you don't do as well as your peers, you'll be called *dull, dumb*, or, to be more politically correct, *a bit on the slow side* or "very nice." And if you are two or three standard deviations away from the mean of the group, you'll be hailed as a "genius" at one end of the bell curve or dismissed as an "imbecile" or an "idiot" at the other, less happy end of the curve. The devising and administration of the intelligence tests turns out to be a notable achievement of psychological measurement, but also a perilous one.

As a scholar, having settled on a noun, I also needed a definition of what constituted an intelligence. Over the years, I have tinkered

1. Writing in 2020 I note that US President Trump often defines individuals in terms of their intelligence or IQ or lack thereof. See https://www.multipleintelligencesoasis.org/blog/2019/6/4/trump-and-iq and Valerie Strauss, "Howard Gardner, Father of 'Multiple Intelligences' Theory, Unpacks Trump's Narrow View of Intelligence," *Washington Post*, February 1, 2017.

with the exact wording of that definition. But in *Frames of Mind*, first published in 1983, I put forth my thinking in informal terms: "A human intellectual competence must entail a set of skills of problem solving—enabling the individual to resolve genuine problems or difficulties that he or she encounters, and, when appropriate, to create an effective product—and must entail the potential for finding or creating problems—hereby laying the groundwork for the acquisition of new knowledge" (62).

Looking back nearly four decades, I am relieved that I was appropriately modest in my claims for the definition and the criteria of an intelligence: "Ultimately it would certainly be desirable to have an algorithm for the selection of an intelligence . . . at present, however, it must be admitted that the selection (or rejection) of a candidate intelligence is reminiscent more of an artistic judgment than of a scientific assessment . . . where my procedure does take a scientific turn is in the making public of the grounds for the judgment, so that other investigators can review the evidence and draw their own conclusions" (*Frames of Mind*, 63).

I had thrown down the gauntlet: Goodbye, or even good riddance, to a single intelligence as probed by the ubiquitous IQ test; greetings to multiple intelligences, modes of assessment yet to be determined. I would soon see how the world would react to the words and claims in the new and perhaps daring synthesis that I was putting forth.

Let me step back for a moment.

As I mentioned at the start, this memoir differs from most instances of that genre. It's not really a personal memoir, nor is it a complete autobiography. It focuses on my ideas—especially the theory of multiple intelligences—and on an analysis of my own mind, which, I contend, is a synthesizing mind. Until this point, as I proceeded from my childhood to the emergence of MI theory, I have proceeded largely in chronological order, from Scranton to Wyoming Seminary to Harvard, from history to Soc Rel to developmental psychology and neuropsychology, from young scribbler to a writer in various genres.

In the remainder of the book, I continue to describe ideas and events and, as appropriate, give the dates of the occurrence. But as my focus shifts, from the development of MI theory to the reception of it in the academic and public worlds, and from the development of a synthesizing mind to an analysis of its workings and products, I will deal with themes from the last half of my life with the narrative proceeding thematically rather than chronologically.

And though the book makes no effort to be personal—it's not about my love life or my political views—it's important to mention crucial events that occurred at what Dante termed "the middle of life."

In November 1981, I received a phone call from Gerald Freund, who headed a recently launched program at the Chicago-based MacArthur Foundation. Like many other academics I had heard of the Prize Fellows program, nicknamed the "genius award," and had even expressed an interest in studying those who had received the award. And I knew—because he had told me—that a University of Indiana linguist named Thomas Sebeok had nominated me for the award. Nonetheless, since I am rarely optimistic about anything, I had not expected to receive the award, at that time $196,000, tax free, spread over five years, with all medical expenses covered.[2]

---

2. Today the comparable award is $625,000, without those enticing extras.

Receiving the award changed my life. When I received that call, I had tears in my eyes and heaved a huge sigh of relief. I had been raising money for my salary for the preceding decade and I was tiring of this precarious lifestyle, as was my family. Equipped with this windfall in money and the associated prestige, I went to see the dean of my school, Patricia Graham, who had succeeded Dean Ylvisaker. I told the dean that if I could not be made a professor in five years, I would move to another campus. This was scarcely a threat; at haughty Harvard, such a speech act would not have any effect, unless it were a negative one. But Dean Graham saw it to it that within five years, I did indeed become a professor, giving me a new and far more permanent descriptor to add to my name.

I should also share the most personal part of my life. With Judy Krieger Gardner, whom I'd met and fell in love with right after college and married less than a year later, I had three children: Kerith (1969), Jay (1971), and Andrew (1976). Judy was a wonderful person, widely admired by colleagues and friends. Whatever incompatibilities we may have had were at least as much my fault as hers. But in the early 1970s, I met Ellen Winner and we fell in love. After much soul searching, I made the decision to seek a divorce—without question, the most painful experience I've ever had, one that inflicted pain on the whole nuclear and extended family, and one that still makes me shudder when I think about it. (For decades I could not watch movies or television shows about divorce.)

Ellen and I married in 1982 and in 1986 we adopted Benjamin, then an infant, from Taiwan. Judy and I were able to coparent and Ellen became a wonderful stepmother. Then, in 1994, Judy died unexpectedly and tragically of a brain aneurysm, and the family again had to reconfigure. I believe that we succeeded in this endeavor. Like my other children, Ben is now grown up and married, and his daughter Olivia (child of Ben and Genie) joins Oscar and Aggie (children of Jay and Jeanne) and Faye Marguerite and August-Pierre (children of Andrew and Vanessa). Family has always been the most important thing in my life. Perhaps for that very reason, I wanted to keep it apart from what is a scholarly, and not a personal, memoir.

REACTIONS TO MI

In the introduction to this book, I relate an episode about a lecture—memorable to me—that I delivered shortly after the publication of *Frames of Mind*. Until that time, I was a promising young researcher in developmental psychology and neuropsychology. Though I lacked regular employment, I was able to eke out a living through grants at Harvard Project Zero, housed at the Harvard Graduate School of Education, and at the Boston Veterans Administration Medical Center, affiliated with the Boston University School of Medicine. A competent synthesizer, I also was an author of textbooks, books for the general public, peer-reviewed articles, and occasional essays and reviews in the popular press. From time to time I would teach a class at Harvard, at nearby Clark University, or, one summer, at the University of Toronto. But from 1984 on, for better or worse, indeed for better *and* worse, I was the "MI" person.

When you publish a book in the United States, you first notice whether *anyone else* notices the book, and since tens of thousands of books are published every year, getting noticed at all is a considerable, nontrivial achievement. There is no question that *Frames of Mind* was noticed. It was widely reviewed, and for the most part quite favorably. Reviewers realized that, even if the idea of a single intelligence measured by a single standard test was flawed—and public intellectual Walter Lippmann had made that argument persuasively sixty years before—no one, and certainly, no psychologist, had put forth and developed the idea of several distinctive forms of intellect. Equally certainly, no one had defined, named, and provided criteria and empirical evidence for multiple intelligences. Especially for a lay reviewer writing for a general interest publication, it was not easy to take issue with a four-hundred-page book with hundreds of footnotes emanating from a scholar associated, if precariously, with prestigious institutions.

I've often remarked that the *good thing* about MI theory is that you can summarize it in a sentence: "This guy Gardner claims that we have seven separate intelligences, called the multiple intelligences." Of course, that's also the *bad thing* about the theory: it's easy to draw many erroneous conclusions from a single sentence summary of a massive tome. As I might put it in the language of this memoir, it's possible to provide a very brief synthesis, but that synthesis could easily be misleading. Indeed, scans through textbooks in the fields of psychology and education reveal numerous inadequate summaries and misleading syntheses of MI theory.

In addition to largely favorable reviews in the print media, broadcast media also took a heartening interest. Nowadays, if a book like mine were to get any broadcast attention, it would likely be discussed on National Public Radio in the United States and possibly foreign outlets like the BBC. But decades ago, in a different, less diffuse, and (in my view) more thoughtful, media climate, I appeared frequently on television, including the desirable morning talk shows, like the *Today* program on NBC. For a scholarly tome, that degree of visibility would be most unlikely today.

Within a year of publication, I was approached by the British Broadcast Corporation. Martin Freeth, a producer of TV documentaries, wanted to make a seven-part broadcast series, each part focusing on a separate intelligence. Work on this project, named *Lifelines*, went quite far and I lined up various scholars, personalities, and venues to be featured on the program. For a while I fancied the possibility of becoming a television personality, on the order of astronomer Carl Sagan, or, more probably though less popularly, my Harvard elder colleague, economist John Kenneth Galbraith. (See the cover of the brochure for the series in the second group of photos.)

But eventually the project fell apart. A new producer replaced Martin Freeth, and he wanted to change the list of intelligences, alter my role to a commentator rather than the host or "presenter," and, most dramatically and annoyingly, fix my teeth and have surgery performed on my wandering eye! I decided to withdraw from the project. This decision shocked the BBC personnel, and there were transatlantic flights in both directions in an effort to get me to change my mind. One does not lightly turn down a television series on "the Beeb," as it was nicknamed. But I was firm in my decision and have never regretted it. I was beginning to realize that one cannot easily control what it means to be "captured by MI theory."

So, in a manner of speaking, I was becoming famous—or, at least, better known and more gossiped about.

Then, within a few years, reviews and critiques began to appear in scholarly publications. There was considerable agreement that I had introduced a new way of thinking into that strand of psychology that focuses on cognition, on intellect, but there the consensus ended.

Those scholars who had some distance from the psychological study of "intelligence" and from "psychometrics" were generally sympathetic to my undertaking. I would call them "respectful." In contrast, those scholars who were closer to the psychological study of intellect were quite critical, and sometimes viciously so. From their perspective, Alfred Binet's original idea about testing intelligence, and the century-long efforts by measurement experts to codify and standardize his idea, represented one of the primary achievements of psychological research and application in the twentieth century. There were many tests of intellect; they correlated reasonably well with one another; and, of signal importance, if someone was a good performer on a test of one intellectual feat, he or she would likely perform well on another test—the aforementioned "positive manifold" among cognitive tests. And IQ was essentially fixed: your intelligence at age four at least roughly predicts your intelligence at forty and beyond.

Now suddenly, someone from the outside appeared—not a member of the club, not deeply immersed in psychometrics, not a tenured professor anywhere—claiming or purporting to undo the achievement and the consensus of scores of researchers over scores of years. This guy Gardner threatened to knock down the edifice of intelligence, the house of IQ, that had been carefully constructed over the decades. And he was doing so, not with a new set of tests, either validated or at least susceptible to validation, but by drawing on motley evidence from different cultures, different vocations, different historical and prehistorical eras, and even from different parts of the brain—the latter pursuit being dismissively labeled "the new phrenology."

Over the years, these and allied critiques have continued, testifying both to the robustness of the MI ideas *and* to their proclivity for annoying the hell out of "real" or mainstream psychologists. In addition to numerous disparate critical articles and talks, there is now an entire volume called *Howard Gardner Under Fire*. In its four hundred pages, several psychologists chip or chop away at MI theory and I do my best to respond—respectfully, but also with evidence and argument.

Let me list what I consider to be the most voluble (if not the most valuable) criticisms of the theory and indicate how I have responded to them:

MI theory is not empirical. These critics are confusing *empiricism* with *experimentalism.* It is indeed the case that I did not create a test of multiple intelligences. Nor did I carry out experimental research to ascertain to what extent performance in one intellectual sphere correlated with, was independent of, or actually interfered with performance in another sphere. In the case of MI theory, I have not been an experimentalist.

But MI theory is based almost entirely on empirical findings—findings from a range of fields (e.g., anthropology, genetics, neurology, sociology) and findings from a range of populations (e.g., prodigies, savants, those living in nonliterate societies). It is a wide-ranging work of synthesis. And if the theory were to be changed—as indeed it was, when I added the naturalist intelligence, and contemplated other candidate intelligences—it would be changed on the basis of new empirical evidence, and not on a whim.

MI theory is "old hat." Earlier card-carrying psychologists like L. L. Thurstone and David Wechsler had either described other intelligences or dissected IQ into its components. This claim is true in the sense that I was far from the first person to suggest that there might be a "social intelligence." But no one had laid out an ensemble of intelligences and described their provenance and their operations in some detail. Some psychologists had mapped out levels of intellect, with some levels being more capacious, and others more specialized or targeted. I tip my hat to my predecessors John Carroll and J. P. Guilford, but these taxonomies are either based entirely on existing tests (Carroll) or are largely conjectural (Guilford). My set of intelligences derives from a synthesis of information from several fields, and thus is the product neither of numerous psychological tests nor of the imagination of an eminent psychologist.

What counts in life is IQ; all else is a sideshow. Without question, on the whole it's better to have a high IQ than a low IQ, just as it's better to be healthy, and of height and weight within a standard deviation of the norm. But—and this is a crucial aspect of MI theory—IQ is important to the extent that the tasks one has to perform at work and in other spheres of life *resemble* those posed in a generic IQ test. And so, to be concrete, if you are going to work in an educational setting (as teachers and researchers do), then IQ is a good prognosticator of the level of competence you'll reach. At least *pretty* good; once you move into the ranks of management, then other skills and other liabilities come into play and perhaps come to the fore. But if one looks at what one needs to succeed in non- or less academic realms such as the arts, athletics, politics, psychotherapy, sales, or seduction, then the predictive value of IQ alone is sharply reduced.

Furthermore, proponents of this "IQ über alles" or hegemonic position can be hoisted on their own petard. First of all, over time, what we test to determine IQ changes. The items change: tests no longer ask for definitions of words that are more familiar to those from higher social classes or what is the right thing to do in certain privileged situations. The kinds of items also change. For instance, the Raven's Progressive Matrices test is based entirely on the completion of an ordered series of visual patterns—no words, just geometric diagrams.

More importantly and more critically, the IQs of entire populations themselves change. Over recent decades, manifesting the so-called Flynn effect, the average IQ of populations in many societies has gone up a full standard deviation. In lay terms, it's the difference between being average and being dull, or being average and being sharp. And so, both what is measured in IQ tests, and how performances change over time, operate as a kind of a brake on the "IQ über alles" perspective.

It's worth remarking that a "multiple intelligences" view is often disturbing to academics. Members of the scholarly trade valorize that particular and perhaps peculiar blend of language and logic that is a hallmark of scholarly research and discussion. But that situation can change abruptly when an academic happens to have a child with one or another learning difficulty. Such situations have been known to produce an instant convert to MI theory: "My child may not do well in school, but he is a great camper," or "She has a deep understanding of others" or "She is musically intelligent."

What Gardner calls intelligences are really talents. Call them what you like, but if being good with music or spatial thinking is a talent, then so is being good with math or language. Call them all talents, or call them all intelligences.

But as noted, in all likelihood, I would not be writing, and you would not be reading, these words, had I written a book called "The Theory of Multiple Talents." Within the Anglo-European language community, talents proliferate, whereas intelligence has been seen as unitary and exalted. And so, it was by picking a fight with prior vocabulary, and with traditional conceptualization, that I changed, or even dramatically altered, a long-running conversation. In the future, people may speak about social intelligence, or emotional intelligence, or bodily intelligence, without giving the expression a second thought, let alone using quotation marks or footnotes.

There are multiple intelligences, but not the ones described by Gardner. Probably the chief other contemporary critic of standard IQ theory is Robert J. Sternberg, a widely recognized and highly prolific psychologist of our time. He failed intelligence tests when he was young and, perhaps in revenge, devised his own test in seventh grade (see chapter 2). At roughly the same time that I was developing MI theory, Bob Sternberg was developing his *triarchic* theory of intellect.

As signaled by the determinedly academic name, Sternberg divides intellect into three components: a knowledge acquisition component, which enables one to process information; a metacomponent, which allows one to plan and monitor the processing of information; and a performance component, which actually carries out the processing of information. Sternberg also writes about *successful intelligence*: the ability to identify life goals, evaluate one's strengths and weaknesses, and then attain those goals. In addition to the analytic components, successful intelligence also entails creativity, practicality, and wisdom.

For the purposes of textbooks and popular articles, my work is often grouped with that of Sternberg, who is a colleague and friend. But in fact, the two lines of work are quite different. Sternberg's triarchic theory is based on standard items in tests of intelligence; it identifies and dissects the processing capacities that allow (or preclude) high performance on such instruments. It's entirely "inside baseball." Also in contrast with my approach, his notion of successful intelligence lumps intelligence together with capacities that I have studied, such as creativity and ethics, but ones that I have deliberately parceled off from intelligence.

Another difference is that Sternberg's formulation is blind to content. That's to say, the components and metacomponents operate on information, whether it be numerical, musical, spatial, or personal. But for me, *content is the heart of the matter*. According to my analysis, we don't process music in the same way as we process numerical or spatial or personal information. Nor does memory for one kind of content reliably predict memory for other kinds of content. Whether you can remember text passages does not predict how well you remember musical themes or geographical routes, or how someone mistreated you at last year's Thanksgiving gathering and, accordingly, how you felt in the ensuring hours or days.

Yet another difference between our theories is probably less apparent to outsiders. Sternberg sees himself as a psychologist addressing other psychologists, and his stock value (in his own mind, if not in the minds of observers) varies with his niche within the discipline of psychology. By training, and perhaps by modes of thinking, I am also a psychologist. But I think of myself as a lapsed psychologist, as a systematic social thinker, and above all, as I argue in the concluding chapters of this book, as a synthesizer of knowledge about human beings and the human mind. And then, for most of the rest of the world, I am an educator, or educationalist, and, for better and worse, I am likely to remain so.

So far, I've described how MI theory was initially received by general readership and was subsequently critiqued by fellow psychologists. But the promulgation of MI theory in the early 1980s occurred at a time when related events were happening in the academy and in the wider world.

In the academy, the early 1980s saw the height of interest in the work of linguist and cognitive scientist Noam Chomsky and those who were strongly influenced by his ideas (as was I). Indeed, in 1981, when I published a second edition of *The Quest for Mind*, my 1973 study of Jean Piaget and Claude Lévi-Strauss, I added a section on Chomsky's structuralist work, with his approval. I also embarked on a history of cognitive science, a field in which Chomsky played a vital founding role. Most important for my purposes, Chomsky was quite open to the idea of separate "mental computers." In 1983, the year that *Frames of Mind* appeared, Chomsky's close colleague Jerry Fodor published a book called *The Modularity of Mind*. Though proceeding from linguistics, philosophy, and computer science rather than from psychology and the softer social sciences, Fodor also took a pluralistic view of the different modules of mentation. I benefited from this intellectual and scholarly zeitgeist. A "multifaceted view of mind" was in the academic air, so to speak.

I was also a beneficiary of a heightened interest, in the United States and abroad, in the quality of education for young people. In 1983, again the year *Frames of Mind* was published, a report commissioned by President Reagan appeared with the provocative title "A Nation at Risk." According to this report, American K–12 education was in very bad shape. Indeed, as captured in a memorable phrase in the document, it was as if a rival nation, by crippling our schools, had committed an act of terrorism. Counter to Reagan's own expectations and aspirations—the president actually had wanted to use the report as a means of *eliminating* the federal Department of Education—the report's authors concluded that it was high time for the federal government to assume a far more active role in enhancing student motivation and achievement.

While housed at a graduate school of education, I had hitherto not been deeply involved in K–12 education. But in the mid-1980s, I became much more engaged in what was happening in American classrooms and also in various policy initiatives. Soon my own work was enriched and extended by the opportunity to try out various educational ideas that were related to multiple intelligences.

MI IN THE WORLD

Though I had grown up in eastern Pennsylvania, I had never heard of the small town of Kutztown. In 1985 I was invited to a meeting on arts education to be held at a branch of the state university located in that community. Since my parents lived relatively close by, I readily agreed to drive down from Massachusetts to attend. The invitation came from Patricia Bolaños, an arts teacher in Indianapolis.

Only when I met Pat Bolaños did I learn that she had driven, with a half dozen of her colleagues, all the way from Indianapolis to meet with me—a trek of fourteen hours! And then I encountered yet another surprise: she (as prospective principal) and her colleagues had decided that they wanted to launch their own elementary school. It would be a progressive public school, it would foreground the arts, and it would be built around the idea of multiple intelligences. They proposed to name the school "The Key School." While they sought my permission to launch the school, I made it clear from the beginning that the decision was theirs. As I put it at the time, "I think that this is an exciting idea, I'll try to be helpful, but *you* are the K–8 educators, and it is *your* school."

For the next decade or so, I made regular trips to Indianapolis to visit the school, to observe what was happening, and, on occasion, to offer suggestions. Even over and above my deficit in recognizing faces, I don't find it easy to get to know other people. But I was at Key so often, and was so fascinated by what was happening there, that I came to feel part of the "Key family," a phrase that we frequently used. It's fair to say that I came to know the Key School—its faculty, its program, some of its students, and a few of their families—better than the schools that were attended by my own children.

If you had asked me—or, for that matter, others familiar with MI theory—what an MI school would look and be like, you'd have gotten a variety of answers. There's no evident path from a four-hundred-page scholarly volume to a bricks-and-mortar educational institution. I doubt that any outsiders would have come up with the same answer as did Pat Bolaños and her fearless "Key eight." (Yes, we picked up an additional teacher along the way.) With appropriate teachers, students took courses in the several intelligences, even complete with the names "bodily kinesthetic," "linguistic," and so on. In the music class, everyone learned to play the violin. In addition, each day included "pods," or extracurricular interest groups in which students could putatively make use of their favored intelligences in their favorite ways. Pods included such topics as cooking and gardening as well as activities like designing buildings and making money. Students were expected to launch, develop, and publicly present individualized projects that reflected their passions and their blends of intelligences. All of the activities were recorded by Sandy Sheets, a full-time videographer, who remained with the school for two decades. The capacious report cards documented student progress across the spectrum of intelligences.

For a while the Key School could do no wrong. Families flocked to it; parents and students were generally pleased with their experiences; a large foundation in the area, the Lilly Endowment, provided vital additional funding; the school was featured on national television, in national and international publications, and was selected by *Newsweek* magazine as one of the ten best schools in the world. Even conceding that this label was hyperbolic—after all, how could one possibly make such a determination?—for a time, the Key School was clearly a landmark on the educational landscape.

Given the widespread and ever-widening interest in Key, my colleagues and I at Project Zero decided to carry out some research on site. We were particularly interested in what it took to create, execute, and then evaluate projects that putatively drew on the multiple intelligences of school children. And so we worked with the staff and students to create "rubrics"—the technical name or "ed speak" for scoring systems. Through careful application of these rubrics, we could evaluate students' projects in a systematic way. I had become interested in the possibility of evaluating students in terms of their productive work and play, rather than via their scores on conventional standardized tests. Accordingly, I devoted considerable effort toward the creation of student portfolios—collections of projects, and the work that went into their realization. I also coined the term "processfolio" to call attention to the important work of planning and revising carried out *en route* to a finished display. Again, much of this process was recorded for posterity by Sandy, the talented and ubiquitous videographer.

Clearly this experimentation was of interest to elders, teachers, administrators, and occasional visitors and journalists. But what of the students themselves? From all I could observe, most of them were thriving in this more casual, more varied, and more pointedly experimental setting. One day I had an experience that moved me. Without any advance warning, so far as I could determine, the school was visited first thing one morning by an internationally known violinist, Dylana Jenson. The K–2 youngsters were called into the auditorium to meet Ms. Jenson and to hear her perform short pieces—some familiar to American ears, others quite musically adventurous.

With amazement, I beheld these young students. They watched assiduously and listened attentively in rapt silence. And after the performance, they asked good questions. I had seen young children at artistic performances in many places, and except for elite schools in China, I had never seen such a dutiful *and* engaged audience of five- to seven-year-olds. At that very special moment, I realized that Key was accomplishing something rare and important—involving young people "from the get-go" in significant artistic experiences, indeed significant learning experiences. I would bet a fair sum that those who attended Key for several years became "music aficionados for life."

This growth and concomitant celebrity were not without pain. Neither the Indianapolis school board nor neighboring communities and rival schools were pleased at the publicity that was given to the experimental and idiosyncratic Key. Indeed, the link to Harvard and to my "theory" was probably a dual-edged sword.

Jealousy is a prepotent human motivation. To mark the fifteenth anniversary of the school, I and other friends and supporters gathered at a big celebration held in an auditorium at the state capital. Many political and educational leaders paid tribute to the Key School's educational accomplishments. At the end of the evening, Principal Bolaños rose to address the audience. She concluded her remarks with these pointed words: "Most of all I would like to thank the five Indianapolis superintendents with whom we at Key have worked over the years. *Without your steadfast opposition*, we would *never* have achieved what we have achieved."

While this remark was meant partly in jest, it was also very much on point. The celebration probably represented the zenith of Key. The local situation was changing. There was less money for public schools (and certainly less money for experimental public schools), and more of a division between the "have" and the "have not" segments of the local citizenry. The national situation was also changing, with increased pressures for standardized testing, core curriculum, and one-size-fits-all classroom protocol.

Sadly, Pat Bolaños developed brain cancer at around this time. After a heroic year in which she attempted to carry on with her work (and even honoring her speaking engagements at far-flung sites), she succumbed to this illness. In the decade following Pat's death, the school continued and indeed, as Pat had dreamed, the community even added a high school. I remained in loose touch with the school; several of the original eight pioneers would come periodically to Cambridge, and we'd have a drink and wax nostalgic. But it came as no surprise to anyone when the Key School officially closed a few years ago. In reality, it had been *in extremis* for some time.

Few take pleasure at the death of an institution, particularly one that has had positive effects on many people over a considerable period of time. But I've come to think of such a situation in a somewhat different way. Especially in the United States, the land of "voluntary associations" in Alexis de Tocqueville's memorable phrase, most institutions have a limited life span. In some cases, their demise is due or even overdue. Moreover, Key was conceptualized and brought to fruition by an unusual leader during the brief time span in the United States when educational experimentation was encouraged—even in staid Indiana.

What's ultimately important is not the longevity per se of an educational institution, but rather the number of individuals who were affected favorably while they were involved in the institution, as students, parents, teachers, visitors, or other personnel. Perhaps even more important is what happens to individuals who once spent time at the institution—a week for a visitor, or five years for a music or fifth grade teacher, or K–8 for a student—where they *go* and how they *think* and what they *do* thereafter. I suspect that, like a few other powerful institutions with which I've been fortunate to be associated (Jerry Bruner's development of the social studies curriculum "Man: A Course of Study" leaps to mind), the spirit and practices of Key live on with many people in many places, spread far and wide. That rule of thumb may even apply to new concepts and constructs like multiple intelligences: they do their work, the relevant "memes" circulate, and then they are absorbed into the cognitive woodwork as their initial sources and explicit terminology fade into oblivion.

Scarcely a year after Key opened, I was once again contacted by an educator, Tom Hoerr, the youthful principal of an elementary school in St. Louis, Missouri. Tom was another innovative educator who wanted to make use of MI ideas. He suggested a visit and some consultation. As had happened with Key, I was intrigued by the idea and delighted to visit with Tom and his colleagues. While I did not visit St. Louis as regularly as I had visited Indianapolis, I came also to know the New City School, its key personnel, and its philosophy quite well.

This school differed from Key in many ways. To begin with, unlike Key, New City was a private school—its survival depended on tuition and gifts. Nor was there a Lilly Endowment down the street to replenish the trough periodically. It also had a more focused age span of K–5. Private schools also attract a somewhat different faculty than do public schools. For example, private school faculty are less likely to have been enrolled in teacher training institutions, and more likely to be willing to sacrifice salary in return for other perks. And in the case of private schools, there is no teachers' union.

From my perspective, as a researcher and educator, there were other more significant differences. Rather than launching a new school, Tom proposed to guide an already existing school in new directions. For many months, the teachers read and talked about MI ideas, among themselves and occasionally with me, to consider the best ways to refashion and incorporate some of them into the sinews of the school. Rather than changing the curriculum or the schedule per se, the goal was to introduce MI ways of thinking into the thought processes, the daily routines and rituals, the "DNA" of the community. Especially crucial was the notion that each individual—young child or mature adult—is different; each has his or her preferred interests, ways of interacting, and ways of knowing. And especially distinctive, and especially important, were the personal intelligences—how you know yourself, how you know others and interact with them in ways that are appropriate, considerate, and ethical. Indeed, as much as New City was moving toward becoming an MI school, it was equally appropriate to think of it as a "school for the development and nurturance of the personal intelligences."

New City gained its share of local and national publicity. Like Key, it attracted a seemingly endless stream of visitors from around the country and, indeed, from much of the globe. It also garnered interest in other ways. Unlike the leading figures at Key, Tom and some of his colleagues were writers. They produced books and shorter publications, detailing what they were doing, why they were doing it, and with what effect. Consistent with their background in the arts, Key educators had highlighted visual communications, such as videos; consistent with their more traditional educational backgrounds, New City educators favored the written word. As if to highlight that trait, in 2006, they created the first "multiple intelligences library." I had the privilege of "cutting the ribbon," so to speak. Tom Hoerr also became a national expert on various aspects of education, appearing in person in many venues, and writing regular columns and books for educational organizations, most prominently the Association for Supervision and Curriculum Development. As I write, his "MI newsletter" has been going strong for twenty-seven years! And while he stepped down as principal of New City in 2016, the school has so far remained a viable institution—a much happier fate than befell the Key, located in another metropolis in the Midwest.

For at least a decade, I reveled in the interest in MI, especially from real educators in real places. I received many invitations to speak about the ideas themselves, and about their educational implications, from sites around the nation and, increasingly over time, around the world. Fortunately by now, thanks to Dean Graham, I had a day job, teaching cognitive and developmental psychology at the Harvard Graduate School of Education. (I also taught elective courses in creativity and the arts.) But if I had not had such a niche, I could easily have kept quite busy just responding to these requests; and if I had wanted to, I could have commodified MI.

The decisions *not* to create MI curricula or MI schools or MI merchandise was a fairly easy one for me to make. I do not have much of a commercial streak in me; to paraphrase a famous remark by President John Adams, "My father was a businessman, so I did not have to become one." But this also turned out to be a prudent decision. Had I succumbed to that temptation, I would have wanted to be successful at it, and that aspiration would have consumed a huge amount of time, without any guarantee that the time would have been well invested and adequately compensated. Even more important, I'd have had to create and protect the brand—sticking to things that "worked" in the commercial sphere, periodically introducing new products, gimmicks, slogans—whether or not I had any interest in doing so, or even believed in the value of such deliberately designed manipulations. Both by inclination and by virtue of my training as a scholar in the 1960s, such pursuits would have been abhorrent to me. In fact I believe quite strongly that ideas developed by scholars should be available freely, and for free, rather than being monetized and commercialized. Sometimes my kids tease me and say "Dad, you could have been rich!" But in truth, our family is comfortable and, in comparison to many people with much more money than I could ever dream of, I possess something invaluable—"enough."

So although I did not take the "for profit" route—or, for that matter, the "prophet" route—I did continue to have a significant investment in the health and provenance of MI theory. From a scholarly point of view, I embarked on a number of research projects, such as the aforementioned study of portfolios undertaken at the Key School. To give the flavor of the kinds of enterprises MI spawned, I'll mention a few.

Artistic knowing. In conjunction with the Educational Testing Service (ETS), my colleagues and I developed new forms of assessment. We measured ways of producing, perceiving, and reflecting in the arts. (Perhaps overly fond of acronyms, we called this endeavor Arts PROPEL.) These efforts, which spanned the visual, musical, and dramatic arts, proved useful in evaluating assemblages of student work; and to the extent that American educators, as well as those from other nations, elect to focus on student work over time rather than simply on test scores and final grades, they can build on the foundation that we created in the late 1980s.

Practical and creative intelligences. Working with my long-time colleague Robert (Bob) Sternberg (the scholar who had put forth an alternative view of intelligence), my team and I carried out two projects in middle schools. One was called "practical intelligence for school (PIFS)" and the other was called "creative intelligence for school (CIFS)." The effort was worthwhile: we combined two influential approaches to intelligence, worked with a targeted audience, and created materials that could be used "off the shelf." The collaboration also added to our list of book and articles directed toward education. But from my own point of view, the collaboration was not notably successful. While the research teams (from Harvard and Yale, respectively) got along personally, and had comfortable meetings and enjoyable meals at various places, our intellectual orientations and our styles of work were incongruent, if not baldly at odds. Personal symbiosis and intellectual syntheses are two different matters.

Assessing intelligences of young children in a comfortable setting. If asked for the most important research effort to stem from MI theory, I would unquestionably nominate Project Spectrum. Back in the days when I was developing MI theory, my closest scholarly colleague was David Henry Feldman. David was the then youthful scholar, mentioned in passing (on page 96), who in the early 1970s was offered the job at Yale for which I had applied. He was the first to speculate that MI theory would disrupt the hegemony of IQ. In the course of several conversations, David and I concluded that if MI ideas were to have influence beyond scholarly and intellectual chatter, it would be good to have some means of identifying and assessing the *intelligences* of children.

We decided to launch an assessment project with young children. We chose this "target" population for at least three reasons. First, while a doctoral student I had taught K–2 children; second, at the time that "MI" was becoming widely known, we both had three young children; and third, the Eliot-Pearson Children's School at Tufts University, where David was teaching, had a nationally recognized preschool.

We dubbed our endeavor Project Spectrum. Rather than simply creating seven tests for seven intelligences (bringing to mind the old musical *Seven Brides for Seven Brothers*), we instead worked to develop an MI classroom milieu. We wanted students to have the opportunity daily to work with inviting materials whose "affordances" would presumably stimulate the various intelligences. Accordingly, the "Spectrum classroom" was richly equipped with musical instruments, building blocks, space for gymnastics and dance, toys with which to build stage sets, dioramas, and enact simple stories, tools to manipulate in various classroom spaces or to create or repair materials, and the like.

In one sense, such a classroom does not represent that much of a stretch. Progressively oriented preschools, whether in the Montessori, Froebel, Dewey, or Reggio Emilia mold, may well resemble a Spectrum classroom. But the Spectrum classroom was also distinctive. We provided an area where researchers could inconspicuously observe the children at play. We also created targeted measuring devices in the guise of play materials; these measuring devices allowed us to look more directly at an intelligence-in-isolation or at intelligences-in-combination. These instruments included board games where we could monitor and tease apart mathematical and interpersonal intelligences, and a large block space where the children could re-create the classroom in miniature (spatial intelligence) as well as indicate what they themselves had been doing earlier in the day (*intra*personal intelligence) and what the other children had been doing alone or with one another (*inter*personal intelligence).

Ultimately, we evaluated each student's intelligences in two ways. First, we observed them in free play over a significant period of time to see which intelligence area and materials they favored, in which ways they used them, and, in particular, whether their use became more sophisticated over time. These were "observed intelligences." But we also created instruments that could be drawn on to examine intelligences in a more focused and less messy way. These were "measured intelligences." And we were able to record each child's "spectrum of intelligences" at a given moment in time and then revisit it a year later to see whether that spectrum had been altered in a noticeable way.

As mentioned, Project Spectrum stands out among all the MI-related enterprises in which I have been personally involved. We showed that it is possible to measure intelligences in a natural setting as well as in a relatively structured milieu. We were able to write "Spectrum reports" on each child that made sense to the teachers, parents, and (we hoped) the growing students. With our committed colleagues Mara Krechevsky, Jie-Qi Chen, and Julie Viens, we wrote three books on Project Spectrum. These volumes, still in print, have been translated into several languages.

Still, I would say that Project Spectrum is primarily an *existence proof*: a demonstration that a posited psychological entity is not simply the conceit of an imaginative scholar. We showed that intelligences can be operationalized, and that information on their distribution across individuals can be codified and shared with others. In the absence of a "Spectrum central" (or a Spectrum "seal of approval"), it's up to others to determine whether these materials are useful to them and, if so, whether and how to tweak them. I suspect that, as with other educational ideas that enter the market place, some schools that call themselves "MI" sites would not satisfy my own standards, while other sites, which would impress me, have neither heard of MI or of me.

Other measures of MI. I would be remiss if I did not mention that others have created their own MI instruments. Indeed, if you Google tests of multiple intelligences, you will encounter many of them. I've been asked to endorse various of these tests but have not done so. By far the most widely known is Branton Shearer's MIDAS test. This test is in many ways ingenious and has been used in many places for many purposes. Yet it is at heart a self-report test. As such, it is limited by the accuracy of one's own knowledge of one's own strengths and limitations—it's more a test of intrapersonal intelligence, or, in less happy circumstances, of intrapersonal ignorance.

Assessing intelligences at all ages in a natural setting. I had given up my search for an authentic and convincing measurement of the intelligences across the age span until, around 2005, I received some intriguing information. I learned that in a town in Denmark named Nordborg, a company named Danfoss (which makes heating and cooling devices) had set up a theme park that featured a facility called Explorama. The park was built around the concept of multiple intelligences. I was invited to the opening of the facility, but couldn't attend. However, within a year or so, I made the trip to Denmark and met the Clausen family who had underwritten the Explorama. And then I spent the better part of a day walking around the Explorama at a theme park called Danfoss Universe.

By the time the visit was concluded, I had experienced an amazing "aha." At long last I had encountered a site that could actually be used to assess intelligences in an "intelligence fair" way across a wide span of ages (from five to fifty and perhaps beyond). The Explorama consists of several dozen games and challenges that each person can approach in his or her own way. There are musical and linguistic signals to be listened to, reproduced, and altered in specific ways. There are spaces to be explored by one's whole body, or by one's own hands—and if one violates the strictures of the space by bumping inadvertently into a part or zone that is off the indicated track, a noxious sound blares forth. There are board games that tap numerical, logical, and interpersonal capacities. And so on.

Perhaps the most ingenious game requires two persons to spin separate dials in order to move blocks across a space so as to hit a target (thereby drawing on bodily and spatial intelligences). To accomplish this task effectively, members of the duo need to coordinate their adjustments of separate dials, which requires interpersonal intelligences as well.

I thanked my hosts for in effect fulfilling my dreams for an ecologically valid assessment of MI—and without any direct input from me. Then came a lament: "But we haven't figured out how to measure intrapersonal intelligence." I thought for a while and came up with an idea: "Before a person enters the space," I suggested, "why not give her a list of tasks, described in sufficient detail so that she can imagine them? And then ask her to predict how well she will do in each. If her predictions are accurate, she will have displayed one variety of intrapersonal intelligence. And if she is wildly off the mark—well, then you've given her something to work on."

Whether or not this idea was implemented, formally or informally, I was pleased that I could make at least one relevant suggestion that could be implemented by the architects of the Explorama.

Collaborating with individual and organizations in MI issues. One feature of my work and my life is "No wasted time." Or, to quote once again the great European economist Jean Monnet, "Regard every defeat as an opportunity." While I love working with my long-time colleagues at Project Zero, I have found that collaborations beyond our circle tend to be challenging.

Accordingly, few years ago, in an effort to understand *why* collaborations like PIFS and CIFS are so challenging, or indeed, why the Early Symbolization Project had never been completed, Wendy Fischman, Lynn Barendsen, and I launched a project called "good collaboration." We ultimately identified eight elements that characterize good collaboration. To aid memory, the eight elements constitute an acronym:

Excellently Executed
Leadership Driven
Engaging for Participants
Mission Focused
Ethically Oriented
Nurtured Centrally
Time Well Spent
Solution Inspired

Whether or not this scheme proves helpful to others, we ourselves have found it useful in determining whether or not to launch a collaboration and, far more difficult, when to *terminate* such a collaboration. We might say that we try to make use of interpersonal intelligence at the group or organizational level.

Clearly MI launched many ideas and many projects. Branton Shearer, the creator of the MIDAS test, had the idea of assembling a group of those who have worked with MI ideas in the practical sphere. Accordingly, in 2006, a solid dozen of us presented a symposium at the American Educational Research Association in New York City. Shortly thereafter, Jie-Qi Chen, Seana Moran, and I edited a book with the grand title *Multiple Intelligences around the World*. In that hefty document, forty-two scholars from fifteen countries on five continents describe a variety of enterprises—classrooms, schools, museums, theme parks—for a variety of constituents—young students, college students, gifted students, students with learning disabilities, job seekers, those with free time and disposable income—which draw on the ideas of multiple intelligences. When scholars and practitioners approach me with questions about how best to implement "MI" ideas, I refer them to this handy resource.

In any reasonable sense of the lexicon, MI was by this time well "on its way." There were positive examples of schools with which I had worked personally, as well as numerous examples of schools, parks, museums, and other institutions scattered around the world. If I so chose, I could have rested on my MI laurels. But as I was to learn to my regret, not all of the examples were positive. Once you launch a meme in the wider world, particularly one that can be easily summarized if not synthesized, you simply cannot control its trajectories.

PUTTING MI IN ITS PLACE

In 1993, I received a message from a colleague in Australia. The message was simple and stark: "Your ideas are being used in Australia, and you aren't going to like the ways in which the ideas are being used."

I was intrigued. This was already in the days of email; but if attachments were in play by then, I did not know how to download them. So I asked the colleague to mail me the materials about which he had expressed alarm. And so he did.

I remember standing in my office, then in an upgraded Longfellow Hall, reading through the documents. My colleague in Australia was right: I did *not* like the way in which my ideas were being used. In what I've come to think of as "the smoking gun," I beheld a chart of the various ethnic and racial groups in Australia, along with an indication of *which* intelligences they were *strong in* and *which* intelligences they *lacked*. To top it off, the chart made recommendations about how students in each group should accordingly be treated or taught.

I was stunned. If we had adequate measures, there may well be some differences in average profiles of intelligences across groups—perhaps men versus women, perhaps Asians versus European, perhaps introverts versus extroverts. But certainly, the variation *within* any "demography" would overwhelm any differences *between* "demographies." Even if such group differences were found, we'd have no idea of what caused them and what interventions might lessen them, make them vanish, or even reverse them.

These contentions emanating from Australia were clearly pseudoscience. And worse than that, the unwarranted claims were being mobilized to indicate which kinds of educational interventions were appropriate and, by implication, which were not. Clearly my ideas were being exploited to justify unwarranted educational interventions—throughout an entire state, perhaps even throughout the whole nation.

What to do? It took little agonizing on my part. I was approached by broadcasters in Australia to offer my views on these recommended interventions. I agreed to appear on *The Sunday Program*, roughly equivalent to the widely watched and discussed *Sixty Minutes* in the United States. I declined to comment in any way on the motives of the educational planners; I had no idea who they were nor "where they were coming from." But I stated resolutely that there was no evidence that these claimed group differences were in fact true and that, accordingly, I could not support any of their educational recommendations. Other experts also appeared on the show and weighed in with their reservations. To my great relief, the proposed educational intervention was discredited and ceased to be used. But while I had not obsessed about the decision to denounce the educational intervention, I realized that I had to pay *far more attention* to the ways in which my ideas were being used—and, alas, misused or abused—and to intervene when it seemed needed or appropriate.

As an academic, my first impulse was clear: I should write about this experience. Two years later, in a wide-circulation educational journal, I published an article titled "Multiple Intelligences: Myths and Realities." It is my most cited article. In that essay, I laid out a set of *mis*understandings of MI theory that had come to my attention, and tried to set the record straight.

Some of these I've already mentioned. For example, many observers felt that if there are seven intelligences, there should be seven tests—a proliferation of IQ tests, as it were. (Marketers rubbed their hands in anticipatory glee.) To be sure, I had no objection to assessing intelligences per se, as with Project Spectrum and the theme park in Denmark's Danfoss Universe, both described in the preceding chapter. But I believed that paper-and-pencil tests were completely inappropriate for gauging most of the intelligences. Also, answering yet again the critiques of some psychologists, I tried to explain, as patiently as possible, that while the theory is not *experimental*, it is most determinedly *empirical*. And, indeed, further empirical evidence might cause me to posit additional intelligences—which I eventually did—or to reconfigure the current array—which I have not done, at least not yet.

Other of these corrections were on the technical side. I sought to explain the difference between an *intelligence* (a computational capacity of the brain) and a *domain* or *discipline* (a set of practices featured in a culture or society). Put concretely, the capacity to move one's whole body or parts of one's body in a deliberate and skilled way entails an intelligence: bodily kinesthetic intelligence. But the culture in which one lives determines whether and how one expresses that intelligence: through sports (and, if so, which ones, boxing or fencing or jai alai); or through dance (and, if so, which form—ballet or polka or hora); or through fine motor movements (and, if so, via sewing or typing or tying knots or playing the harp); or, less happily, only for certain demographic groups or not at all.

As yet another example, I pointed out that MI theory contests not the *existence* of general intelligence (technically called "g") but rather its provenance and explanatory power. That is, across any battery of paper-and-pencil tests, a common factor is likely to emerge upon statistical analysis. But the size of that common factor, the so-called *positive manifold*, depends on numerous variables, including *which* tests we include, *how* we score or weight them, *which* statistical analyses we use, and, interestingly, the composition of the population *to whom* we present the battery.

Phi Delta Kappan, now shortened to the *Kappan*, the journal in which I published this "course correction," is addressed primarily to educators. And so it is hardly a surprise that the points on which I spent the most time and spilled the most ink had to do with educational misunderstandings. I'll summarize the two major points here.

There is no single MI educational approach. Many educators, often with the best of motivations, believe that there is a single educational approach based on MI theory. And sometimes (indeed, most times) these educators believe that *they* know what it is. For example, the staff of the Key School believed that there should be a class devoted to each intelligence; in contrast, the staff of the New City

School believed that education should focus on the personal intelligences. Some believe that I, as the creator of the theory, have indicated how best to use MI theory or ideas in the classroom, and that I am the sole possessor and bestower of the "MI seal of approval."

But as I took pains to point out, MI theory is a set of scholarly claims, based on a synthesis of a vast amount of data and concepts drawn from numerous sources. The theory could be right or wrong, modified or not. In any case, one can *never*—I repeat *never*—go directly from a scholarly theory to a set of educational practices. And that is because education, like a swathe of other human activities, entails value judgments. Before you can draw on any empirical claims, you have to decide *what you want to achieve and why.*

To give an example: As the "MI guru" I am often asked whether one should teach to build on existing strength or to bolster areas of weakness. I respond that one can do either or both. But *which* course one elects to follow is based primarily on what *you want to achieve* with an individual, a group, or indeed with a population as a whole. If personally pressed, I might continue: Be broad with younger children (stimulating the less strong intelligences) but increase the focus on the stronger intelligences in the case of older adolescents (building on documented strengths). I also point out that your decision may well depend on a family's socioeconomic status and prospects. If the family is very comfortable, a youthful member of that family can afford to cover the waterfront, to be a jack of all intelligences, or, if you prefer, a "renaissance child." In contrast, if an indigent extended family depends on the child for eventual economic support, it makes more sense for the growing youngster to develop the stronger intelligences as effectively and efficiently as possible.

Or as I sometimes put it: Tell me *your* educational goals—achieving high scores on a validated test, having a democratic community, developing leadership skills—and *then* we can work together to ascertain appropriate uses of MI theory. But if you believe that you want to achieve *all* those goals equally, it's better to go back to the drawing board, armed with an effective eraser. In an effort to achieve all aspirations, you are likely to fail across the board.

Terminology matters. Multiple intelligences are not learning styles! This injunction concerns a practice that have I found particularly galling. Quite apart from my work, several scholars had spoken and written about *working styles* or *learning styles*. I have no objection to the terminology per se—I do not consider myself a language policeman—and there may well be reasons for embracing such terminology.

In fact, however, many educators—and, again, they could be perfectly well meaning—speak of *intelligences* and *styles* as being identical or interchangeable. This I cannot abide. For one thing, such individuals speak about someone as having a "visual" or an "auditory" learning style, and I find this labeling scientifically ungrounded and conceptually confused. Here's why. Individuals who have trouble reading are often called "visual learners" because they gravitate toward pictorial or graphic imagery rather than toward text; but of course, reading is visual as well, and these individuals are singled out precisely because they *cannot* read easily. Or others are called "auditory learners," but of course, both speech and music are perceived auditorily, and rarely are both sources of information examined when such claims are made.

Adding insult to injury, those who take a "learning styles" perspective often assume that if a person approaches an experience one way, she will necessarily approach other experiences in the same way. But I know from observations, and from research, that one can be quite planful or playful with one kind of content—say, language—while being quite the opposite with another kind of content—say, spatial or bodily information. Or to be vividly self-referential, my books and files are well organized, while the top of my desk and the floor of my study are a mess. (See the second set of photos!)

I must concede that my occasional attempts to insist on terminological distinctions have not been particularly successful. Many educators and laypersons continue to collapse intelligences and styles, but I still try to enforce the distinction. As with other aspects of the "MI life" or "life after MI," it's difficult to abandon the effort altogether.

So let me step back and attempt to characterize *what happened.* Based on years of research, I had carried out an ambitious synthesis of human intellectual faculties. Individuals, especially educators, had read the original synthesis or brief summaries of it, or simply heard about it in one way or another. Based on their own understandings or misunderstandings of what I had written, these presumably well-intentioned individuals had attempted to draw lessons about themselves, their work, or, most often, about the education of others.

MI theory had come to resemble an item from a Rorschach test: *individuals saw in the MI inkblot what they wanted to see.* And while I often did not see the same thing, I had only limited power to correct their vision and to suggest another, more faithful "reading" of the blot. I often think of a line attributed to famed anthropologist (and master synthesizer) Margaret Mead: "In education, the American public needs a new plaything every ten or fifteen years. It doesn't much matter what it is!"

When I mentioned to one of my students that I was writing about the theory of multiple intelligences and how it affected my life, she posed astute questions: "Are you happy or sorry that you came up with idea? And if you are ambivalent, do you wish that you had come up with it earlier in your life, or later in your life?"

In fact, a salient motivation for writing this book has been to provide perspective on the role of MI in my scholarly life, describing how that synthesis of almost forty years ago has affected me and quite a few others, ranging from professors to pundits to parents to passersby, who happen to read or hear about the idea.

I have moved on from MI and pursued many other projects, interests, and opportunities, but it remains the theory for which I am best known. Each week, sometimes each day, I get several letters about MI. Perhaps half of these communications ask for help in setting up MI programs or courses in a school or some other institution. On rare occasions I can actually make a specific recommendation. For example, if you are interested in early childhood, read the three books about Project Spectrum; or if you are working in the Philippines, you should learn about the international MI school in Manila. Sometimes, I can refer the correspondent to a colleague or former student who has interest in MI and may have the time to offer more than a few words of appreciation, encouragement, or help.

The next largest category of "over the transom" correspondence entails specific questions. In articles, books, and on my MI website (with the evocative name "multipleintelligencesoasis"), I provide the answers to several dozen FAQs. If the query cannot be answered simply by pointing to one of these resources, and if I have the time, I try to provide an answer or at least indicate how I would go about trying to answer the question.

The final set of communications that I receive regularly consists of invitations to speak. Even now, decades after the ideas were developed and described in publications, I am still principally known for and asked to speak about MI. In truth, I have little desire to deliver yet another address on MI. I've spoken and written myself out on the topic. And so, unless it's a favor to a friend, I simply say no and, if appropriate, refer them to a small group of colleagues who are able and willing to give talks on the topic.

Even though MI is not at the center of my radar screen, it would be misleading to suggest that my thinking about the theory has not changed.

First of all, to the original seven intelligences, I've added an eighth: the *naturalist intelligence* (think Charles Darwin). In brief, this is the intelligence that allows humans (and perhaps other species) to make distinctions in the world of nature, between one animal (perhaps a predator) and another (perhaps prey), among plants, clouds, rock configurations, and so on. Clearly, the naturalist intelligence was important prehistorically, as humans lived long or died suddenly by virtue of what they daily ate, cultivated, or spurned. Nowadays, in any developed country, most of us secure our nourishment by shopping at markets, be they small or super. But whenever we select one pair of shoes rather than another, one SUV rather than another, or one head or variety of lettuce rather than another, we make use of the naturalist computational machinery that allows us to make fine distinctions within a category.

I have also toyed with the addition of two other intelligences. One candidate is *existential intelligence*: the intelligence that allows humans, though probably not any other species, to pose and ponder big questions about life, death, love, war, indeed existence itself.

The second candidate is *pedagogical intelligence*: the intelligence that allows humans, though probably not other species, to teach skills and convey information to others, both those who are quite knowledgeable and those who are far less in the know.

My reluctance to add intelligences derives directly from the method that I initially used around 1980 to identify the seven intelligences. I reviewed massive amounts of literature and organized observations and findings in a systematic way, determining whether these findings met or lacked the eight explicit criteria of an intelligence. During a 1994–1995 sabbatical year, I had sufficient time to carry out this exercise with respect to the naturalist intelligence. It has clearly earned its place on the final list.

But I have not had the time, or, to be candid, the inclination, to consider adding further intelligences. And so, while, with a wink, I allow others to speak of pedagogical and existential intelligence, those candidate intelligences have not become part of my intellectual synthesizing enterprise. They have not received the Gardner seal of approval: they remain in intellectual or terminological purgatory or limbo, so to speak.

In the original search for intelligences, I drew on available information about brain organization and genetics. I believed, and still believe, that there is a firm biological basis for each of the intelligences. But in recent decades I have not had the time or the expertise to monitor and synthesize this burgeoning literature. And to my regret, MI per se has not attracted the sustained attention of researchers in the biological sciences. Colleague Branton Shearer has devoted considerable effort to the neurosciences of multiple intelligences, and his conclusions, sympathetic to the theory, have now been published. I also continue to monitor the work of neuroscientists like Evelina Fedorenko, Olivier Houdé, and David Somers, who study the relationship among, and possible independence of, different cognitive and perceptual capacities.

So, we might say that while I have maintained an "MI shop" in recent years, it has not featured any new product lines, nor have there been interested buyers in the wings. Many have offered me the opportunity to codify and monetize the idea of multiple intelligences, but as I mentioned earlier, I have rejected all such requests.

However, the idea of multiple intelligences has stimulated a variety of commercial undertakings around the world. In Macao, mothers are encouraged to buy pasteurized milk in order to raise the intelligences. A chain of hotels in Hispanic countries offer play areas for stimulating the intelligences. An advertisement for sleek German automobiles portrays its features as different intelligences—the motor as evidence of naturalist intelligence, the self-driving feature a manifestation of mathematical intelligence. Dozens of educational companies around the globe feature products yoked to the strengthening of one or more intelligences. Perhaps most flagrantly, several countries in South and East Asia claim to be able to discern particular intelligences by an examination of fingerprints, a pseudo field called dermatoglyphics. (Half of those who write me about fingerprints and MI are horrified by the claim; the other half who write me assume that it's true and won't be dissuaded from this nonsense.) For a while, I tried to dampen this commercialization—in one case, Harvard University actually sued the malefactors. But life is short.

In 1995 the MI train, still chugging along, took a sudden and unexpected turn when Daniel (Dan) Goleman published a book called

Emotional Intelligence. In his book he argued that, in addition to IQ, another kind of intelligence proves crucial for success in the world. As the subtitle provocatively announced: "why it can matter more than IQ."

As I understand it, the book initially had decent but not remarkable sales, until *Newsweek* magazine, at the time a well-respected and highly influential weekly periodical, featured the book on its cover, with the pithy abbreviation *EQ*. And from that time forward, the cause of "emotional intelligence" took off like the proverbial rocket and has scarcely slowed down in the intervening quarter century.

Dan Goleman had been a graduate student in psychology at Harvard shortly after my own stint in William James Hall. Thereafter he had become an excellent science reporter for the *New York Times*, at the time when that area of journalism was still relatively new. He covered several of the sciences and had generously featured my own work, particularly my interest in the two personal intelligences. I do not know whether or to what extent emotional intelligence (EQ) would have been discovered and so named without my own previous work—or, for that matter, the research of psychologists Peter Salovey and John Mayer. That answer remains unknown to me—and, I suspect, to Dan himself. It does not matter, for I am pleased with the attention paid to his work and in no way begrudge it.

This train of thought prompts an amusing story. Though I had been invited to South America in the 1980s and 1990s, I had never traveled there. Finally, in the summer of 1997, I decided to undertake a speaking trip to several countries, accompanied by my son Andrew, who spoke Spanish (which I do not). When we got to

Brazil, in particular (where, of course, the principal language is Portuguese), I was frequently asked to sign books, and several times, I was asked to sign Dan Goleman's book. This annoyed me, because, of course, I am not Dan Goleman and I have my own ideas, and my own books, about intelligence. I often thought to myself—though I don't think I ever said it aloud—"You don't ask one painter of water lilies to sign the canvas of another painter of water lilies." But when I returned home, I found that my Brazilian publisher had tripled the advance on my next book about the intelligences! Any hard feelings were quickly assuaged.

Often, I'm asked about whether I "believe in" emotional intelligence. The answer is largely yes. I don't use that term, because as far as I am concerned, emotions accompany any and all intelligences; emotions are not a separate realm, cognitively speaking. Much of what Dan intends by his term is covered by my "personal intelligences," inter- and intra-. From the very first, I have insisted that these two intelligences are far more closely intertwined than any others. To underscore the point, in *Frames of Mind* the two appear together in a single chapter called "The Personal Intelligences."

But there is another difference, one that grows directly out of the good collaboration project and its concomitant insights. When Dan Goleman speaks and writes about emotional intelligence, he gives it a positive spin. And indeed, in the opening pages of his first book on the topic, he writes evocatively about a personable New York City bus driver, and the warm feelings and connections that the driver engenders in his passengers on a muggy summer day.

I'm all in favor of emotional intelligence, but I insist on thinking of it—and indeed thinking of *all* intelligences—in an *amoral* way. The same capacity that enables the driver to make passengers feel good could also be used to manipulate them or even to torture them. It's the *uses* to which an intelligence is put that determines whether it is benevolent or malevolent.

I remain in touch with Dan Goleman who, like me, has gone on to write about many more topics, including ones much closer to the ethical sphere. But far more so than I have, Dan has continued to work with those who build on his ideas about intelligence. And he holds positions and directs or advises entities that feature his pathbreaking formulation. I think it is fair to say that "emotional intelligence" is closer to his daily consciousness than "multiple intelligences" is to mine.

Also, and Dan can claim far more credit for this than I can, in the aftermath of the enormous publishing success of his books on EQ, an entire industry of different kinds of intelligence or intelligences has been posited, spawned, and monetized. You see it in bookstores, even more in airport terminals: sexual intelligence, leadership intelligence, moral intelligence, cooperative intelligence, business intelligence, and so on . . . and so on. When giving talks on MI, I sometimes project slides of various book covers, with their respective emblazoned "intelligence" names. I conclude with a slide on "financial intelligence" and then quip: "That's the only one you really need. Once you have financial intelligence, you can buy all the others."

It's also fair to say, I think, that Dan has had no more success than I've had in moving the psychometric community or the psychometric needle. Most psychologists of intelligence are as skeptical of emotional and social (and moral and spiritual) intelligence as they have been of MI theory. Indeed, because Dan's success has been so public, academic psychologists may beat up on him more than they beat up on me. The fact that psychologists John Mayer and Peter Salovey (the latter now president of Yale) have created measures of emotional intelligence does not seem to help. As an early reviewer of *Frames of Mind* noted, trying to change psychologists' views of what intelligence is—and how to measure it—is like trying to move gravestones in a graveyard.

The world in which psychometricians live is simply different from the world in which educators or businesspeople or, indeed, the rest of us live. Though neither MI nor EQ is likely to earn a place of honor in college textbooks, they are too salient in the public culture to be ignored. In my terms, they are scholarly syntheses that have "changed the conversation."

Though the analogy is far from exact and may be seen as self-serving, I cannot help but mention psychoanalysis. The ideas developed by Sigmund Freud and his followers, including my own esteemed teacher Erik Erikson, have never been accepted by much of the psychological community. And in some cases, that rejection is legitimate. Concepts like the Oedipus complex or the death instinct, and stages like the anal stage and the phallic stage, do not stand up to scrutiny, let alone to systematic experimentation. They may say more about Vienna circa 1900 or Freud's own personal psyche than about "human nature" from prehistory onward and in diverse cultures scattered around the globe.

But Freud's discovery of unconscious mechanisms and processes and the importance of dreams, and Erikson's concepts of life stages and of the identity crisis, capture something significant about human nature, or at least human nature as we have observed, dissected, and conceptualized it in modern times. In the lexicon of this book, I call this "changing the conversation" or proposing a "convincing synthesis." As the poet W. H. Auden eulogized on the occasion of Freud's death: "He is no more a person now but a whole climate of opinion."

To be sure, one never changes the conversation completely or permanently. Many people, for good or not so good reasons, want to continue the old conversation, be that a belief in a single intelligence or in a mind devoid of unconscious thought. But like casual conversation among friends or neighbors, scholarly conversations continue to change. Sometimes they retrace old ground, but, in the happier circumstance, they can engender stimulating new ideas, new concepts, new directions, new insights. And that is certainly what I hope will happen with some of the ideas and movements with which I have been associated.

Howard's tutor, psychoanalyst Erik Erikson.

Patricia Graham, dean and mentor.

Susanne K. Langer. Photographs of Dr. Susanne K. Langer by
permission of the Estate of Susanne K. Langer.

Mr. Howard Gardner,
Quincy House H 8,
Harvard University,
Cambridge 38,
Mass.

EDMUND WILSON REGRETS THAT IT IS IMPOSSIBLE FOR HIM TO:

READ MANUSCRIPTS,

WRITE ARTICLES OR BOOKS TO ORDER,

WRITE FOREWORDS OR INTRODUCTIONS,

MAKE STATEMENTS FOR PUBLICITY
  PURPOSES,

DO ANY KIND OF EDITORIAL WORK,

JUDGE LITERARY CONTESTS,

GIVE INTERVIEWS,

CONDUCT EDUCATIONAL COURSES,

DELIVER LECTURES,

√ GIVE TALKS OR MAKE SPEECHES,

BROADCAST OR APPEAR ON TELEVISION,

TAKE PART IN WRITERS' CONGRESSES,

ANSWER QUESTIONNAIRES,

CONTRIBUTE TO OR TAKE PART IN
  SYMPOSIUMS OR "PANELS" OF
  ANY KIND,

CONTRIBUTE MANUSCRIPTS FOR SALES,

DONATE COPIES OF HIS BOOKS TO LIBRARIES,

AUTOGRAPH BOOKS FOR STRANGERS,

ALLOW HIS NAME TO BE USED ON
  LETTERHEADS,

SUPPLY PERSONAL INFORMATION ABOUT
  HIMSELF,

SUPPLY PHOTOGRAPHS OF HIMSELF,

SUPPLY OPINIONS ON LITERARY OR OTHER
  SUBJECTS.

Edmund Wilson's note to Howard.

Cover of the first edition of *Frames of Mind*.

LIFELINES

EXPLORING THE DEVELOPMENT OF HUMAN TALENTS

A MAJOR SERIES OF EIGHT 55 MINUTE FILM DOCUMENTARIES

PRESENTED FOR BBC TELEVISION BY DR. HOWARD GARDNER

Cover of brochure for the ill-fated BBC program *Lifelines*.

David Riesman, professor and mentor.

Research team for the Good Work project, around 2000.

Howard with Good Work colleagues William Damon (center) and Mihaly Csikszentmihalyi.

September-October 1990 | $4.50

HARVARD
MAGAZINE

How Do Children Learn Language?

Psycholinguist Roger Brown has devoted thirty years to understanding this astonishing feat

Brown with research associates Benjamin Gardner, Wolfgang, and Ernie.

Roger Brown on the cover of *Harvard Magazine*, with Howard's son Benjamin.

August 8, 2017

To: Arlie Hochschild
From: Howard Gardner

Dear Arlie,

I don't believe that we have met, though I have known about your work for many years and heard that you made a very successful visit to the school where I teach, some months ago.

Like thousands of others, I found STRANGERS IN THEIR OWN LAND a very powerful work. I've recommended it to many others, and have compared it (to those who have some sociological memory, including Nathan Glazer) to THE LONELY CROWD.

Recently I have started a blog in education. A friend and colleague, Susan Engel, wrote an interesting blog in response to the recently reported Pew finding that Republicans believe that higher education is bad for the nation. Having been immersed in your book, I decided to respond, taking on the voice of a Trump supporter from the deep South. I include a link to the blog post for your possible interest.

https://howardgardner.com/2017/08/08/republicans-are-right-college-matters/

In appreciation and with best wishes.

Howard

August 9, 2017

To: Howard Gardner
From: Arlie Hochschild

Dear Howard,

I remember sitting as a sophomore on the front lawn of the Swarthmore campus, talking to my boyfriend, -- now husband of 42 years—saying, what I'd really love to do is write a book like The Lonely Crowd. So thank you for saying that. And I've long appreciated your illuminating work on multiple intelligences. I'm a fan back. And thanks for your thoughtful blog—we have much work to do.

All the best,
Arlie

Arlie Hochschild's letter to Howard.

Howard's Festschrift
September 28, 2013

The cover of Howard's festschrift. Photo by Jay Gardner.

Howard and his mother, Hilde Gardner.

Howard playing the accordion, around 2000.

The Gardner family in May 2019.

III

UNPACKING THE SYNTHESIZING MIND

ON TO EDUCATION AND GOOD WORK

While MI has been "on maintenance," I've been quite busy with sundry endeavors. Among other things, these activities have given me increasing insight into who I am and what I do for a living. And, as I explore more directly in what follows, they've presented me with new insights into how my own mind seems to work.

One of the privileges—some would say windfalls—of being a scholar is the opportunity to take a summer or a sabbatical leave, travel to an appealing spot, and work on one or more projects. In 1994–1995, at the time that I was drafting my article on the "myths and messages" of MI theory, I had the opportunity to spend a year at the Center for Advanced Study in the Behavioral Sciences, on several attractive acres of land abutting the campus of Stanford University in northern California. By design, I shared this sabbatical year with William (Bill, always) Damon, then at Brown University, and Mihaly (Mike, at times) Csikszentmihalyi, then at the University of

Chicago. Mike and Bill are two well-established psychologists and the three of us were already friends. We respected one another's scholarship but had never collaborated on research. Now we had an opportunity to bring our backgrounds, strengths, and interests together on a proposed project.

At the time Bill was already one of the world's most acclaimed experts on moral development. He had focused particularly on how children's and adolescents' moral development can proceed, courtesy of input from parents, teachers, and the children themselves. Trained as a social psychologist, Mihaly was both an expert on creativity and the inventor of ingenious methods of sampling human experience. Sometime before, he had designed clothing-attached electronic beepers; these devices discharge periodically and allow psychologists to monitor (through self-reports) what a person is feeling, sensing, experiencing, at various times throughout the day. Mihaly was also widely known as the pioneering researcher on "flow," that precious, pleasurable, all-encompassing psychological state where one becomes completely absorbed in what one is doing.

Of course, at the time I was a developmental psychologist and neuropsychologist, focused on cognition. As detailed in Part II, I had become well known for MI theory and had recently been perturbed, even discombobulated, by the frequent misunderstandings and misuses of my ideas.

The three of us had come to the Stanford center with a shared concern. Put simply, we were interested in whether, and in what way, one could be *creative and productive* and yet behave as well in an *ethical or moral* way. These tendencies might pull in opposite directions. Perhaps if you wanted to be creative, you had to toss aside all kinds of ethical and moral injunctions and just pursue your passion. If true, that would indeed be regrettable. Or perhaps it was possible for creativity and morality to go hand in hand. There did seem to be some examples: Charles Darwin in science, Mahatma Gandhi in politics, Pablo Casals in the arts.

Then there's the role of timing: during the moments of creativity, all is allowed or even encouraged; but before one goes "public," other pressures and criteria ought to be applied. Certainly that has been the case with the harnessing of atomic energy and, perhaps, with other enterprises, such as the invention of dynamite, the discovery of DNA and gene editing techniques, the launches of the internet and of the World Wide Web . . . and, looking ahead, quantum computing, blockchain technologies, and the varieties of deep learning and artificial intelligence.

In contemplating this issue, we each had personal stakes. Mihaly's documentation of "flow" as measured by the "beeper method" was often interpreted as something that was desirable in itself and should therefore be pursued as much as possible. But as Mihaly frequently pointed out, a robber cracking a safe may feel plenty of flow; but he or she is not someone whom one should encourage or emulate.

Bill had developed the concept of a "youth charter." This document was designed to help youths and parents work together within a community for constructive ends. Its realization was a time-consuming process, requiring considerable investment as well as flexibility on the part of all parties. But some communities treated the adoption of such a charter as a *fait accompli*; the various stakeholders were unwilling to invest the time and the due diligence to implement it sensibly and, as was often necessary, to correct course. It's easier to state a mission than to realize it.

In my case, as exemplified by the misguided educational intervention in Australia, I had been blindsided. My efforts to document the variety of human intellectual capacities had been hijacked in the service of characterizing differences between cultural groups and implying that these differences were fixed and dictated specific educational interventions. Such endeavors appalled me.

Freed for the academic year, including two summers, of our normal teaching and administrative responsibilities, ensconced in a comfortable and supportive setting, we three middle-aged psychologists had the luxury of time to reflect on those issues, without any requirement to write a specific paper or book. (In our case, those would not have been difficult requirements to honor, because we all like to write—that's how we think and rethink and, with luck and after a few drafts, advance our and perhaps others' thinking.) In the end, after countless meetings and chalk talks and memos, we created a research project, suitably dubbed—or so we thought— "humane creativity," and we sought financial support to carry out that project.

Initially, we sent a grant proposal to six funders, and only one of them—as it happens, the only one with whom we had had *no* previous contact—displayed the slightest interest. I believe that our ideas and investigative methods were insufficiently worked out. Also, to be candid, the phrase "humane creativity" was opaque and off-putting—not favorable descriptors when one is trying to convince a foundation besieged with requests to support a novel endeavor.

Appropriately chastened, we corrected course, worked out adequate data-gathering and analytic methods, and in the end were able to attract no fewer than twenty-five funders. The project became a decade-long sustained effort, involving dozens of researchers on five different campuses. Testifying to the predictable and peren-nial lure of California's benign weather, Mihaly soon moved from Chicago to Claremont in southern California, and Bill from equally chilly New England to Stanford. I stayed put. (During harsh New England weather, I console myself with the thought that as long as my mind continues to wander, I myself can afford to stay put!) Even in the days before Skype, we found ways to keep in touch through frequent phone calls, email exchanges, and memos, scheduling meetings on our three campuses, and ad hoc meetings when our travel schedules coincided or could be tweaked to overlap.

Soon enough, the project became known as the "Good Work" project—a happier and snappier name. While our agenda for understanding the relation between creativity and humane-ness remained, we approached the issue in a more disciplined way. Spe-cifically, we decided to study *individuals in professions*. These could be established professions like law and medicine; aspiring pro-fessions like journalism or K–12 teaching; or pursuits whose pro-fessional status had not yet and might never have congealed such as business, philanthropy, and the arts. We did not fall on one or more swords to defend our assessment of the professional status (or lack thereof) of a particular line of work; but our classification grew out of established sociological criteria for what is, or is not, a profession.

In each case, we carried out in-depth, semistructured interviews of a sizeable number of workers; data collection ultimately involved well over 1,200 interviews in nine separate sectors of work. We read the transcripts, coded and analyzed the data, reflected deeply and collectively on what we learned, and then wrote up our findings for appropriate audiences. These collected efforts ultimately yielded ten books, several dozen articles, and a variety of more practical interventions.[1]

As far as I can recall, I did not consciously use the term at the time, but this was clearly *a massive, collective enterprise in synthesizing*. The situation differed from the Project on Human Potential (see chapter 6), where I was in charge and produced the final synthesis primarily on my own. The Good Work collaboration involved three established scholars in midlife and mid-career, as well as close to a dozen other talented researchers, several with doctoral degrees. Nor did the synthesis occur readily or automatically. We went through several rounds of proposing and revising until we came up with the most comprehensive and satisfying description of what we had learned and the most appropriate terminology and framework with which to introduce it.

You might wonder what it was like for three seasoned scholars to collaborate over the course of a decade. I consider this collaboration to be among the highlights of my professional life, equal in productivity, enjoyment, and learning to my even longer collaborations at Project Zero (now over fifty years) and at the Boston Veterans Administration Medical Center (two decades). Though perhaps demographically similar as middle-aged white male professors in the social sciences, our background and life courses were varied.[2] But we liked and respected one another, willingly discussed and

---

1. These materials are readily accessible at thegoodproject.org.

2. Mihaly, Hungarian by birth, Jesuit-educated, grew up in war-torn Europe; Unitarian Bill, who grew up in Massachusetts, never knew his father; and I came from a close-knit, German-Jewish family transplanted to Northeastern Pennsylvania.

worked out our differences, and have remained close friends. As for the actual writing, I used to quip that Bill provided the rhetoric and the inspiration, I punched out workable drafts, and Mihaly provided context, elegance, and even wisdom as we moved from windy drafts to prose that was ready for publication.

All this before we had developed the Good Collaboration toolkit (see pages 155–156).

I cannot presume to describe the thinking of my senior colleagues, let alone the thinking and researching processes of the more than a dozen younger researchers and research assistants who worked on this project. (See photo in the second group of photographs.) In my case, unlike the work on MI theory, I was not dealing primarily with written sources. Rather, I myself carried out a few hundred interviews of highly esteemed professionals and read all of the other ones. I wrote notes and memos about what I gleaned from each, and I also read and heard the comments of others on the team. Some of the organizing principles were dictated by the research methods and were self-evident: which profession did a subject belong to, and what role did he or she assume; how did subjects respond to various prompts and ethical dilemmas; which questions did they answer, which questions did they raise, which questions did they avoid or stumble over, and did they follow up the interview in any way.

Ultimately, we had massive amounts of data to review and to organize. And here my exercise resembled more closely what had occurred on the Project on Human Potential fifteen years before. I created lists, charts, matrices, diagrams, all in an effort to make sense of what we were learning and convey it to others in ways that were sensible and, if we were lucky, convincing to others as well. In a word, I synthesized. The difference was that my colleagues were synthesizing as well, and in the end, with good natured exchanges and critiques spreading over many months, we came up with terms and analyses that we all found accurate and satisfying.

I can spare you a lot of additional reading and ad hoc synthesizing by describing the basic elements of good work as we have come to characterize it. An individual who carries out good work exhibits three properties: that person carries out the work itself in an *excellent* way, is deeply *engaged* in that work, and carries it out in an *ethical* way; and one does not fully qualify as a good worker unless one is excellent *and* engaged *and* ethical. Conveniently, (in English, at any rate) each of these adjectives begins with the letter *E*. We even have contrived a visual or graphic synthesis with three intertwining strands. They can be captured in a triple helix of ENA, thereby paralleling the canonical visualization of DNA.

Excellence Ethics Engagement

You may be wondering what all this has to do with multiple intelligences or, with Mihaly's concept of flow or Bill's youth charters. On the one hand, the three *E*s can be seen as growing out of our respective scholarly expertises: Bill is an expert on ethics or morality; Mihaly is an expert on experience or engagement; and I aspire to expertise on excellence, or excellences in the intellectual (which includes the artistic) sphere. We have intertwined our expertises, so to speak. But the work also helped us to deal with personal challenges having to do with the multifarious interpretations and frequent misunderstandings and occasional misapplications of our own previous scholarly work.

Put succinctly, from that time on, whenever I have written or spoken about the multiple intelligences, I point out that they are *amoral*—note, not immoral! *Any intelligence can be used morally or immorally.* Both Goethe, the poet, and Goebbels, the propagandist, were masters of the German language, drawing on the same intelligence, so to speak. Goethe used his linguistic intelligence to write evocative literary works, Goebbels to engender hatred of Jewish people and certain other demographic groups. Closer to our own time, both Nelson Mandela and Slobodan Milošević possessed plenty of interpersonal intelligence. Milošević used it to breed ethnic hatred and cleansing; Mandela drew on his personal skills and charms to unite a warring nation with remarkably little bloodshed. At his presidential inauguration, Mandela invited his one-time jailer to sit in the front row—a prototypical example of combining intellect and ethics.

The Good Work project and its offshoots have constituted much of my thinking and research over the last twenty-five years, and the same can be said for the work of Bill, Mihaly, and our close colleagues. Indeed, as we spawned various associated projects, we shortened the name to "the Good Project"—and now, as we seek to update our thinking and extend the work to other parts of the globe, we speak of the Good Project 2.0. But I've been fortunate to be able to work on several other lines of research as well and to write works on a wide range of other topics.

When I first developed the ideas of multiple intelligences, I saw this work as squarely within my chosen discipline of psychology, particularly cognitive and developmental psychology, with a smattering of neuropsychology. Education was literally an afterthought—a topic to be touched on gingerly in one chapter in the concluding pages of *Frames of Mind*. But, as noted in Part II, much of the immediate and enduring interest in the theory came from the sector of education, broadly construed.

And so, cognizant of a sector that was intrigued by my ideas, I began to think and write seriously about education. Initially, and not surprisingly, I drew on my knowledge of developmental psychology; and so my first foray described the "unschooled mind" in a book with that name. I delineated the abilities and proclivities that young children exhibit before they enter formal schooling, and then the challenges and opportunities that await such children as they are placed in a class with others, led by a (hopefully) competent instructor, and invited to master a curriculum and acquire certain skills valued by the ambient culture.

Initially my ideas about education were much influenced by the philosopher John Dewey and by my own teacher and mentor Jerome Bruner, himself a Deweyan. Yet I soon found myself assuming a defiant position. Far from being a blank slate (as philosophers and psychologists in the empiricist tradition have maintained) on the one hand, or a miniature scientist or philosopher (as optimistic authorities have suggested) on the other, the five- or six-year-old child strikes me as one who has already developed ways of thinking that are in many ways *inimical* to the tasks of school. Reading and writing are not simply transcribed listening and speaking; they are complex codes with their own rules and procedures and pitfalls. As a species, we did not evolve over millennia to read and write. These are recent cultural inventions that represent formidable learning challenges, and especially so for a sizeable subset of youngsters.

Pursuing this line of argument, I contend that learning to think mathematically, scientifically, and artistically involve the overcoming, the disabling or dismantling, if you will, of "intuitive ways of making sense." These entrenched ways of thinking may well have had their purposes over the lengthy course of human evolution, but they constitute distinct obstacles to the "schooled mind." Accordingly, *The Unschooled Mind* is filled with descriptions of stereotypes and misconceptions that make "school learning" difficult. We can call these misconceptions the "intuitive syntheses" of the young child: the ways in which the unschooled mind puts together information based on the range of available experiences and, possibly, on some inborn predilections. (Experts on cognitive development argue feverishly about this latter possibility, often designated as "innate knowledge.") As an example, if event B follows event A, then A must have caused B. Or if someone looks and speaks like you, they are good; if someone looks or speaks differently, they are bad. Even college students at select institutions who get good grades in science or social science classes often revert to the misconceptions of childhood once they have handed in their final examinations.

ideas in through certain blends of intelligence, while children B, C, and D will draw on their own favored blends. These more practical applications proved helpful and liberating to educators, who all too often teach challenging materials in only one way: the way in which *they themselves were taught*, or the way in which they themselves originally understood and continue to understand to this day.

In *The Disciplined Mind*, I provided quite specific examples of this approach. I outlined a curriculum focused on just three topics: evolution, according to Charles Darwin; music in the compositions of Mozart; and the Holocaust carried out by the Nazis during the Second World War. I emphasized that these three topics are illustrative only; and only a few persons have failed to note that emphasis. I demonstrated how each of these topics can be presented in numerous ways (*pluralization*): Darwin via experiments in the laboratory or a chronicle of his travels around the Galapagos Islands; Mozart via the plot of the marriage of Figaro or the challenge of setting text to music; the Holocaust via the rise of anti-Semitism or the German defeat in the First World War. Then, to complement this pluralization, I illustrate how one child may learn best through logical analysis, a second child through stories, a third child through hands-on activities or creating works of art (*individuation*).

A third educationally oriented book, and the one that remains closest to my own heart and mind, is *Truth, Beauty, and Goodness Reframed*. The subtitle of the hardcover edition is descriptive—*Educating for the Virtues in the 21st Century*—but the subtitle of the paperback has proved to be far more evocative and, it would seem, all too timely—*Education for the Virtues in the Era of Truthiness and Twitter*.

This relatively recent book happens to take as its title and its text the motto of Wyoming Seminary, my secondary school: *Verum,*

Pulchrum, Bonum. I argue that education beyond the basic litera-cies should have as its principal goals the inculcation of these three classical virtues. First I define each succinctly: *truth* is about the accuracy, inaccuracy, or indeterminateness of propositions; *beauty* is about experiences that capture attention, are memorable, and are worth repeating; *goodness* is about the quality of our relations to other persons, both those who are close to us and those with whom we have a more distant, transactional relationship. I then review the conceptions and misconceptions of each of these virtues that are regnant—pervasive both inside and beyond our educational institutions. Finally, I discuss the challenges and opportunities attendant upon an education that takes seriously the cultivation of these virtues, even or especially at times when they are in jeopardy. And indeed, the three topics of my earlier book, are, respectively, examples of truth (Darwin's theory of evolution), beauty (a Mozart composition), and evil, or the absence of good (the barbarity of the Holocaust).

When I wrote the book, at the end of the first decade of the cen-tury, I had already discerned the threats to virtue-based education posed by certain forms of humanistic analysis—postmodernism, which doubts the validity even of *speaking* about virtues—and cer-tain technologies—the readily available and easily manipulable internet, web, and social media. Indeed, at the time, I was involved in a study of these new technologies, the findings of which were described in a 2013 book, *The App Generation*, coauthored with Katie Davis.

Yet hardly anyone, and certainly not I, had any idea of *how chal-lenging it would be* to remain centered on *any* consistent notion of what is true and what is good in the era of truthiness, Twitter, and now, I feel constrained to add, Trump and Brexit. I continue to lecture and teach on this topic, but have to admit that the challenges to the inculcation of these virtues grow ever greater, and the search for firm ground ever more elusive. Still, as I see it, we human beings have no alternative except to continue to seek and to cherish what is true, what is beautiful, and what is good.

My initial forays into education focused on the preschool years and on K–12 age span. Yet my educational focus gradually shifted upward, in projects ranging from observations of adolescents and their immersion in digital and social media to studies about the attitudes toward work espoused by young people. We found that many adolescents aspired to do good work, but only *after* they had achieved fame and fortune by whatever means available to them. In light of this disturbing finding, I have carried out an ambitious research project with my longtime colleague Wendy Fischman and with the expert advice of another longtime colleague Richard Light. The project examines the sector of nonvocational postsecondary education in the United States.

Members of our skilled research team conducted over two thousand semi-structured, hour-long interviews on ten disparate campuses (I've read them all!). We spoke to incoming students, graduating students, faculty, senior administrators, parents, alumni, trustees, and job recruiters. Our goal has been to propose a viable, data-informed form of higher education—one that goes beyond vocational education; that allows ample space for the pursuit of what is true, what is beautiful, and what is good; and that educates people to cast a critical eye on what is not worthy of those virtuous descriptors. Needless to say, a study like this requires enormous acts of synthesizing.

This study is probably the most challenging scholarly assignment that my colleagues and I have ever undertaken. With any luck, by the time you read these words, our analyses will have been completed, and we will have written articles, and perhaps even published a book on higher education in our time.[3]

From my recent foray into my own juvenilia, I discovered to my surprise that I have been interested in educational issues since my teenage years. In fact, in my high school newspaper, I wrote articles about standardized testing, IQ, the American high school, and, yes, even education in the liberal arts. But had I not put forth the theory of multiple intelligences, which elicited such interest on the part of educators across age ranges and subject matters, I might never have spent the succeeding decades thinking about how best to educate the human mind—or, better, human minds. In any case, this puzzle has become one that I ponder daily and which continues to give rise to new projects requiring reflecting, research design, data collection and analysis, and ultimately synthesis and syntheses.

The logistics of such large-scale data-collection studies deserve some attention. Initially, either alone or with close colleagues, I arrive at a tentative description of what I'm interested in and why. I discuss this possibility with colleagues, especially individuals at Project Zero, where I've spent over a half a century, and where several younger colleagues have spent their entire adult years. Together we assemble a small team that commits to narrowing (or, rarely,

---

3. Our initial impressions and tentative conclusions are recorded in the blog *Lifelong Learning*, available at howardgardner.com and also on various articles posted there.

expanding) the project to reasonable dimensions and to carrying out the project itself, should it succeed in securing funding.

Fundraising is largely my assignment. Over the decades, the sources of funding have varied. Projects have been funded by the US government—chiefly the National Science Foundation, or the National Institutes of Health, or a smaller education agency—large foundations, smaller foundations, individuals of means, and sometimes my own honoraria from public lectures and writings. In preparing this book, I looked back to see how many funders I had approached over the years. This turns out to be over three hundred, with well over one hundred separate funders contributing, if one includes repeat funders. Nothing of any scope that I've achieved could ever have been accomplished without the amazing generosity of so many institutions and individuals . . . and, it should be noted, my own tenacity.

The actual work, of course, varies from one study to another, and I've carried out several dozen projects over the last several decades. But in each case, I meet formally with the research team at least once a week and am in daily conversation much of the time even if we happen to be situated in different corners of the globe. We share ideas, impressions, and intuitions, and try to be as frank as possible without being unnecessarily critical. Often, we work together as we carry out interviews or analyze and interpret data. As much as possible, I try to coauthor or coedit articles or volumes. Sometimes we go beyond writing to creating or participating in "real-life" interventions. As I have long quipped, in an effort to describe Project Zero succinctly, "We develop ideas and try to give them a push in the right direction." If I continue to make a unique contribution to projects as the years pass, it's probably in my capacity to synthesize and to help other to carry out that form of thinking.

I have now described in some detail my modes of thinking and working on several projects carried out over several decades. But, you may well be asking, what about my day job?

Since the mid-1980s I have been a tenured professor at the Harvard Graduate School of Education. In that capacity, I attend faculty and committee meetings, and carry out various tasks as requested both by the leaders of HGSE and by the leaders of the larger university.

Of course, my primary job (through the spring of 2019, at which point I became a research professor), has been to teach courses—primarily to master's students at HGSE, but also to doctoral students and, at times, students from other professional schools at Harvard. Over the decades, I have shifted my department affiliation within the school several times, from "human development" to "arts in education" to "mind, brain, and education" to, most recently, "higher education." My courses are directed, accordingly, to students with those scholarly and professional interests.

By a variety of measures, I am a reasonably good teacher, whether teaching large courses (where live or recorded lectures are indicated, or enrollment-limited seminars where discussion and debate are featured). I take my teaching obligations seriously, read papers quickly but carefully, try to get to know the students, and sometimes continue a relationship with students well after final grades are in.

But in truth, it's in working intensively and extensively with individual students on significant projects—typically *their* projects—that I get my "flow" as an educator. Over the decades I have had the privilege of working on such projects with dozens of doctoral students and dozens of researchers at Project Zero. The projects have ranged across the aforementioned four areas of the school, as well as the scores of research endeavors that have taken place at Project Zero since the late 1960s. When I look over my lengthy list of publications, I remember with pleasure and pride over one hundred individuals whom I have had the privilege of mentoring. To borrow some characterizations from the Good Project, I hope that I have served as a mentor, or at least a frag-mentor, rather than a tor-mentor or an anti-mentor.

I have been paid to teach courses, but when it comes to mentoring (and grand-mentoring) the primary rewards are satisfaction and pride. This memoir is also one way of thanking my own amazing mentors and my wonderful students.

11

MY SCATTERED PURSUITS AND THE MIND THAT CONNECTS THEM

In 1975, I was contacted by Larry Gross, a colleague at another university. Larry knew that I had written *The Arts and Human Development*, and that, in the same year (1973), I had also published a book about *Piaget, Lévi-Strauss and the Structuralist Movement*. Larry wrote to say, "You know, there is someone who has written a book called *The Shattered Mind: The Person after Brain Damage*, and he has the same name as you do."

I did not know how to react. Even though my book *The Shattered Mind* may have represented a considerable leap to an outsider, I had indeed worked for some years on an aphasia ward at the Boston Veterans Administration Hospital, and I felt that I knew enough to write about the effects of brain damage on human cognition. In this, I was following the tradition of the pioneering Soviet psychologist A. R. Luria, and, as noted earlier, anticipating as well the evocative writings of the Anglo-American neurologist Oliver Sacks.

Somewhat shamefacedly, I admitted to Larry that I was guilty of "committing" this additional book.

For whatever reason, I have always been curious. I become interested in things I hear about, read about, or observe as I make my way around the world. I investigate them with whatever means are available. And I like to write about them, both to make sense to myself—how do I know what I think until I have seen what I have written?—and to convey my thoughts to others who may share my curiosity. Why else did I produce a newspaper as early as second grade? Why did I aspire to edit the *Opinator*, that weekly high school publication? And why do I continue to post those blogs every other week, till this day? (Between 2015 and the end of 2019, I have published nearly three hundred blog posts.)

And so it's not surprising to me, though it may have been surprising to Larry Gross and perhaps others, that I, a developmental psychologist interested in the arts, should also have authored a book about the effects of brain damage.

What Larry Gross said about *The Shattered Mind* could well have been echoed a decade later in 1983. I had published *Frames of Mind*—my magnum opus, so to speak—but two years later, in 1985, I published a sizeable tome exploring an apparently remote territory.

For several years before, I had been hearing about a putative new field of research called *cognitive science*. The New York–based Alfred P. Sloan Foundation was pouring significant amounts of money into the support and expansion of this nascent branch of study. And yet when I asked various people "What is cognitive science?" I was unable to secure consistent or convincing answers.

And so, armed with a modest grant from the Sloan Foundation, I decided to search for the answer. As is my wont, I read and consulted widely. The grant gave me the leave and the means to travel around the country, and even abroad, to interview the key players in this emergent field. In the end, I concluded that six once separate fields of study were coalescing into the cognitive sciences. Accordingly, the book contained chapters on philosophy, psychology, artificial intelligence, linguistics, anthropology, and neuroscience—six fields that I sought to master at least at the level of a beginning graduate student. The title and subtitle of the resulting spoke clearly: *The Mind's New Science: A History of the Cognitive Revolution.*

This book allowed me to combine my interests and draw on my talents. I am interested in psychology and the mind, broadly construed; I had at that time already written four books featuring the word "mind" in the title and I would write several more. I also esteem interdisciplinary studies—after all, I was then still mourning the death of Soc Rel and was reluctant to be categorized as representative of a single academic discipline. As a psychologist who studied development over time, and as a lapsed historian or historian manqué, I inevitably consider persons and events from an historical perspective. Perhaps reflecting my brief career as a high school reporter and a college ethnographer, I also like to interview knowledgeable persons. I have become a reasonably skilled interviewer and I like to be timely or *au courant*, and to address issues of the day.

It's worth noting what *The Mind's New Science* lacks. While the cognitive sciences clearly grew from the concepts and technologies that emerged during World War II, I minimize these stimulants in my account. My history in the book is centered on questions raised by Plato and Aristotle in the classical era and by philosophers John Locke and Immanuel Kant in later centuries, and not on the emergence of radar, computers, and spying pigeons in the war. My account is also US-centered, thus minimizing critical developments in England, Scotland, Germany, the Soviet Union, and perhaps other centers of research. Finally, the book is a time-bound capsule in a fast-changing field. By the time the paperback edition of the book appeared, a new approach to computing called parallel distributed processing (PDP) had arisen and had become the research method of choice in several branches of the field. Were one to write a new history of cognitive science or the cognitive revolution, these omissions would have to be addressed. And in my case that would require a lot of retooling of an aging brain! But it may also be that cognitive science, like Soc Rel, is a period piece, an interdisciplinary synthesis of a certain time, and that newly emerging interdisciplinary lines of study—spanning, say, artificial intelligence and genomics—are now at the fore, awaiting the efforts of a younger synthesizer.

The book also reveals something about me. I am much less interested in writing the definitive work, or the ultimate synthesis, than I am in putting ideas and items together for the first time—or at least early in the game. I want to put things together as best I can—the initial tentative synthesis, not the last word—and then move on. In that sense, I am like my teacher Jerry Bruner, who often did the first crucial experiment or demonstration, and then left others to follow—or, to phrase this less kindly, to pick up the pieces. Or like Albert O. Hirschman, the insightful economist who did not hesitate to cast his synthesizing powers widely, and described himself as a "trespasser." I have difficulty imagining what it must be like to be political historian Robert Caro, and to spend decades studying President Lyndon Johnson, or to be literary historian Leon Edel, who spent decades chronicling novelist Henry James. But perhaps these biographers would respond that Johnson or James are worlds unto themselves, much like "the mind" that I have been pursuing for at least half a century.

In the decade following my study of cognitive science, I again allowed my curiosity—the questions that I was posing to myself—to proceed in new and unanticipated directions. Having written about intelligence and intelligences, and being known for my writing about the arts—including *The Arts and Human Development* (1973), *Artful Scribbles* (1980), and *Art, Mind and Brain* (1982)—I was often asked, "Well, what about creativity?" And so I embarked on a study of seven significant creators, each of whom putatively drew on a specific intelligence. My selection was guided in part by what I knew and in part by whom I admired: and so I wrote, in order, about Sigmund Freud (intrapersonal intelligence), Albert Einstein (logical mathematical intelligence), Pablo Picasso (spatial intelligence), Igor Stravinsky (musical intelligence), T. S. Eliot (linguistic intelligence), Martha Graham (bodily kinesthetic intelligence), and Mahatma Gandhi (interpersonal intelligence).

I'm often asked about whether I have a favorite among my books, and I have usually chosen *Creating Minds*, for two reasons. First, I got to spend generous amounts of time exploring the work and the works of people whose company I truly enjoyed. These are seven people whom I would definitely invite to dinner. Second, more so than in my other historical and biographical forays, I took the opportunity to consult original sources. I studied the drafts of T. S. Eliot's poems, the letters of Sigmund Freud, Picasso's original sketches for *Guernica*, and the few surviving kinescopes of Martha Graham dancing. Were I granted a free decade, and good health, I'd love to repeat such delvings into other fascinating minds. And had I the opportunity to broaden the pool, I would choose one that is more demographically diverse and one that spans different historical eras. I had a chance to do this in a modest way as I carried out case studies of Virginia Woolf and Wolfgang Amadeus Mozart, in a small book called *Extraordinary Minds.*

Not all biographical efforts come to fruition. In the 1980s I had come to know a fascinating scientist, D. Carleton Gajdusek. Not only had Carleton won the Nobel Prize in Medicine or Physiology for the discovery of slow-growing viruses; he had additional "lives of the mind" as a brilliant physician, as a synthesizer of knowledge in medicine, and as an anthropologist who had collected and categorized information—and, in particular, medical measures—from individuals in dozens of tribes distributed around the South Pacific. I decided to write a book about Carleton's extraordinary mind, and secured his permission as well as a publisher for the book.

One day, when I was deeply ensconced in reading Carleton's medical journals at Harvard's medical library, one of the staff came over to me and said, with a smirk on his face, "Dr. Gardner, I think you should see this." He showed me a report that Carleton had been arrested for pedophilia, involving a son he had adopted from New Guinea. Carleton was ultimately convicted of sexual misbehavior, served eighteen months of a lengthy sentence and, through a plea bargain, was allowed to leave the United States for the remaining years of his life.

I wrestled with whether I could complete and publish the biography; I ultimately concluded that I could not.[1] And so, while Carleton

1. As an editor said to me, "Howard, you'll need too much mood music."

has since been the subject of both a novel and a biography, I abandoned the project. Presumably forever. I learned once again that
not all promising projects come to fruition. And I had to face the
fact that I can be attracted to persons—and to minds—that are fascinating, and that proclivity may blind me to flaws, including very
serious ones.[2]

My other "reach" was less predictable and yet surprisingly productive. Though, like many of my friends, I had long been a "political junkie," I had not thought much about leadership per se. And
so when the distinguished historian and political scientist James
MacGregor Burns invited me to write a book about leadership, I was
appreciative but readily declined.

Nonetheless, Burns had planted a seed in my mind. I began to
think about leadership, and I realized that I might indeed have
something to say on the topic. So once again, as in *Creating Minds*, I
arrayed a set of figures who were effective leaders—though not necessarily ones I knew much about nor ones I unabashedly admired.
I had some interest in their respective intelligences (typically linguistic and interpersonal), but I chose to describe them in terms
of the narratives they created and the extent to which those narratives were actually realized in their own lives—what I termed the
"embodiment of their stories." Indeed, as I came to phrase it, a
leader is a person who is able to affect the minds, the feelings, and

---

2. In the interests of full disclosure, I should mention that at one time I
received support for research from Jeffrey Epstein. Epstein was a wealthy
investor of considerable charm who funded many researchers in the natural
and social sciences at Harvard and elsewhere; he was eventually revealed
to be a notorious sexual predator. As soon as I learned about the serious
allegations, I declined any further support from him.

the behaviors of others; the most effective leaders tell stories that their audiences want and need to hear, and exemplify those stories in their own biographies, their own being.

At first glance, the list of eleven leaders seemed motley. This curious ensemble was both an advantage and a disadvantage, but there was a method to my madness. Anthropologist Margaret Mead and physicist J. Robert Oppenheimer were primarily academics who nonetheless found themselves in leadership positions. Robert Maynard Hutchins led an influential educational institution (the University of Chicago), and George Marshall led the US Army. Eleanor Roosevelt and Martin Luther King Jr. lacked "official" positions and yet exerted powerful influence on several constituencies. Pope John XXIII used his designated position to institute major changes in the Catholic Church within a surprisingly brief period of time. Margaret Thatcher moved a nation in unanticipated directions with long-term, if quite controversial, effects. Jean Monnet inspired the creation of the Common Market and the European Union. Finally, Mohandas (Mahatma) Gandhi, my personal hero, changed the world in hitherto unimaginable ways during the first half of the twentieth century. One has to hope, through the influence of followers like Nelson Mandela and Martin Luther King Jr., Gandhi's remarkable example can continue to do so in ways that are thoughtful, magnanimous, and peaceful.

Though I was not particularly cognizant of it at the time, these two studies—of leadership and creativity—had also revived a long-time interest of mine. Recall that, as a child, I had photographic portraits by Yousuf Karsh of Albert Einstein and Ernest Hemingway in my bedroom. I doubt that I knew about their lives and works in any detail, but I was already an admirer of individuals who had achieved a great deal in the world. At an unconscious level, I not only identified with these individuals; I also strove to make a mark, as they had. Alas, reflecting the prejudices of earlier times, nearly all of my idols were white men, some Jewish, some not.

From one perspective—and one does not have to squint too hard to adopt this perspective—this pile of interests and writings over a few decades looks like a mess. It looks like I am all over map. "Focus, Howard, focus!" Or, to borrow Isaiah Berlin's terms, "Be less of a fox and more like a hedgehog."

Moreover, if you look at my professional affiliations, they also reflect my own wanderings. Forty years ago, I attended meetings of the Society for Research in Child Development. Thirty years ago, I attended meetings of the Academy of Aphasia and the International Neuropsychology Symposium. Twenty years ago, I attended meetings of the American Educational Research Association and the National Academy of Education. Nowadays, I do not attend meetings of any disciplinary group, though I enjoy meetings of organizations that include scholars from many fields, like the American Philosophical Society, the Cambridge Scientific Club, and the American Academy of Arts and Sciences.

But to be frank, while my sequence of associations may look scattered to others, that's not how it looks to me. I prefer to think of myself as having a lifelong mission, or a small set of missions, and continuing to pursue this overarching endeavor in various ways over the course of decades. But it's scarcely enough to assert this; I need an argument and some evidence.

So, let's go back to my adolescence. My beloved Uncle Fritz had a sense that I would find psychology of interest and, accordingly, gave me that Norman Munn textbook with its depictions of color-blindness. Fritz also modeled how to explore widely while also having a question or specific interest in mind. (While one wanders, it's important as well to have a focus, or at least a few foci.) And, lacking formal higher education, Fritz wandered easily across disciplinary terrains and sectors. As editor of the high school newspaper, I was already writing about educational issues, particularly those that arise in secondary school and in the university. And in the senior seminar at Wyoming Seminary, I enjoyed the panorama of American history and literature, and, particularly, the synthesizing writings of Richard Hofstadter and other historians of wide scope, like Eric Goldman and Vernon Parrington.

In college, I savored the opportunity to take many courses and to audit many more, across disparate fields. Initially I thought that I was headed toward history and law, and indeed would probably have done all right in either pursuit—one plausible response to the "life questions" posed by my aforementioned student and touched on in the earlier chapters of this memoir. But while I would have enjoyed remaining forever in college, it was in the department and field of Social Relations that I found an intellectual home. This "landing" was in part because I liked and admired my teachers, some of whom had been among the founders of the department in earlier times, and some of whom were kind enough to serve as mentors. But it was at least as much because I enjoyed the expansive subject matter and found it comfortable, stimulating, and evocative.

Soc Rel, more ambitiously termed "social science," had really come into its own in the middle of the twentieth century. The scholarly fields of psychology, sociology, and anthropology had hardly existed a century earlier. Their observational, empirical, and experimental methods had been developed in earlier decades of the century. These approaches include systematic ethnographic observations, so-called "human relations area files" that chronicle the behaviors of individuals drawn from over one hundred cultures, psychological experiments and interventions, cognitive tests (IQ) and personality tests (Rorschach inkblot tests, and TAT, Thematic Apperception Tests), and small group observational methods. Perhaps most important, large-scale surveys and the powerful statistical methods for analyzing them have been aided since the 1950s by computers that could replace the painstaking individual data analysis by hand (often done by unacknowledged wives and female students and modestly compensated research assistants). I was exposed to the principal thinkers—Marx, Freud, Durkheim, Weber, Piaget, Lévi-Strauss, Mead (anthropologist Margaret as well as social psychologist George Herbert)—and to many of the individuals who had developed the aforementioned research issues and methods. It was a heady time.

Also, and this is perhaps less widely appreciated, these interdisciplinary undertakings—encountered under such names as social studies, social science, social relations, human relations—proved especially attractive to individuals who had grown up in one culture or subculture but then lived in another. Within the United States, the founders had been men (almost always men, I regret to say) from the prairie, whose fathers were often ministers, who came to universities in large American cities; often studied additionally in Germany; and were struck by the vivid and often profound differences between the cultural milieus to which they had been successively exposed. Across Europe, it was visits to the colonial empire or contact with refugees from war-torn places that broadened the perspective of those who undertook social scientific studies. Efforts to understand this twentieth century's clashing (and sometimes melding) of cultures led scholarly inclined individuals to invent and advance the aspiring social sciences.

I am definitely a product of this tension. My parents (and grandparents, and a slew of cousins, aunts, uncles, and family friends) had been born and raised in Western Europe. They represented the bourgeois culture that had been disrupted, perhaps permanently, by the rise of fascism. I felt and sought to deal with the consequent tensions. In the late nineteenth and early twentieth century, the small city of Scranton had been filled with people that had fled Europe (or the American south) for one reason or another and were trying to make a go of it in a region whose anthracite coal-related industries were rapidly declining: Irish, Italians, Poles, Ukrainians, Welsh, Eastern European Jews, and German Jews encountered smaller populations of Asians, Hispanics, and African Americans from the southern states. Though the waves of immigration had basically stopped by midcentury, anyone—*anyone*—who grew up in the Scranton of the 1940s and 1950s intuitively and reflexively categorized persons whom they encountered in terms of their ethnicity and their religion (there were no atheists, or at least no *admitted* atheists). I am constantly amazed that my children and their friends do not immediately and indeed instinctively figure out the ethnicity of just about anyone whom they meet or read about or encounter in broadcast or social media. As a researcher I cannot help wondering on what basis, if any, today's young people classify individuals whom they meet in person or encounter online.

So squaring the circle, I welcomed the chance for more systematic study, observation, and theorizing about the mental and cultural and social worlds of those around me and those who could be studied. And in my own education I particularly admired those individuals, Erik Erikson and David Riesman chief among them, who were able powerfully and convincingly to make sense of these groups, divergences, commonalities, trajectories, and landing places.

If I could have continued to study Soc Rel formally in grad school, undoubtedly I would have done so. But I had to choose among the several tracks in that department. And my romance with the ambitious scholarly project of Jean Piaget along with the writings and mentoring of Jerry Bruner pushed me toward developmental psychology. If I had to choose a single subfield in the social sciences, this was as good as any. It combined history—of individuals—and the human mind, a perennial interest, dating back to that textbook perused in early adolescence. And it was certainly open to sociological and anthropological forays; the spirit of Soc Rel had not yet fully dissipated. While I found social psychology and some strands of experimental psychology of interest, I rarely felt convinced by studies that purportedly yielded dramatic effects after a short intervention or "treatment"—if an effect could be produced so quickly, I believed, it could also evaporate or be erased with equal speed. I was interested in more gradual and ultimately more enduring changes, indeed developments that took place over years and decades, not months or minutes. Perhaps that intellectual proclivity helps to explain my (to me!) memorable clash with Stanley Milgram in the pro-seminar in social psychology.

Echoing Piaget (and returning to a point made in chapter 4), I felt that I needed *dry land* on which to base my observations of and experiments with children. The logical or algebraic structures invoked by Piaget (and also by Lévi-Strauss and, later, by Chomsky)

UNDERSTANDING THE SYNTHESIZING MIND

In the opening days of Donald Trump's presidency, two books gained considerable attention in the United States: J. D. Vance's *Hillbilly Elegy* chronicled his own emergence from a struggling Appalachian past to his current stature as a well-regarded Yale-trained lawyer embedded in the world of venture capital; and sociologist Arlie Hochschild's *Strangers in Their Own Land* described her five years of fieldwork in the deep South.

Vance's book was worth perusing; but as far as I was concerned, it was just one person's story, lacking powerful wider takeaways. In contrast, I particularly resonated to Hochschild's book. And so, while I did not know her personally, I nonetheless wrote Hochschild a fan letter. I indicated that the book had reminded me of

David Riesman's *The Lonely Crowd*—without doubt one of the most influential sociological studies of the United States.[1]

To my delight, Hochschild wrote back almost immediately. She recalled, "I remember sitting as a sophomore on the front lawn of the Swarthmore campus, talking to my boyfriend—now husband of 42 years—saying, what I'd really love to do is to write a book like *The Lonely Crowd*." And now, she had! (See the letter in the second group of photos.)

This exchange got me thinking. What Hochschild did in her book, what we've tried to do in the Good Work project, and more recently, in our study of higher education, goes *well beyond journalism*. This is not meant to critique journalism—a pursuit at least as important as scholarship in academic disciplines. But journalists have deadlines; they write according to assignment and specification; and as soon as one article has been completed and posted, the journalist, like a case-burdened lawyer, necessarily moves on to the next. Even when journalists write books, they typically work like reporters or essayists and not like academics, whose relatively glacial pace of work and fastidiousness about quotations and sources might drive journalists crazy.

In contrast, once past formal training, those of us who are scholars typically select our own topic and spend the time (and as needed, and as available, the money or other resources) examining something systematically. We pursue the topic in as many ways as appropriate and feasible, and seek to relate it systematically to

---

1. I often write fan letters. They are sometimes answered, sometimes not, but the important thing is to bear witness—to write and post the letter and hope that it is not treated, by program or by recipient, simply as spam.

previous work in the field. We never know in advance when we will be done, and it may well be the case that at the end of the day (or, indeed, the decade), we don't find much of interest or we don't have confidence in what we think or believe that we have actually found. And so we may write it up, or not. Just as my adviser Roger Brown had a drawer of unpublished articles, I have several boxes of incomplete books—the biography previously mentioned about virologist Carleton Gajdusek, another emerging manuscript about Mozart—and other projects, such as the projected BBC series *Lifelines* or the aspiring complement to Piaget's study of his three children, the Early Symbolization Project.

This combination of wandering for quite a while, and then sharply focusing—the warp and woof of synthesizing—is what sociologist David Riesman (and colleagues Nathan Glazer and Reuel Denney) did in *The Lonely Crowd* and what Arlie Hochschild did in *Strangers in Their Own Land*. Shifting to psychology, it is what my teacher Erik Erikson did in *Childhood and Society*. And, with apologies for any hubris, it's what Katie Davis and I attempted to do in *The App Generation*.[2] And drawing systematically on copious amounts of data, it is what political scientist Robert Putnam did in *Bowling Alone* and what Daniel Kahneman did in *Thinking, Fast and Slow*. It's what Mihaly Csikszentmihalyi, Bill Damon, and I sought to accomplish in *Good Work*; and what Wendy Fischman and I are seeking to

2. Note that the title is patterned after David Riesman and colleagues—an attempt to characterize an entire age group. And note equally the subtitle: *How Today's Youth Navigate Identity, Intimacy, and Imagination in a Digital World*. Those three "I" challenges are taken directly from the middle life stages introduced by Erik Erikson.

accomplish in our analyses of over two thousand interviews of the various stakeholders involved in higher education.

For sure, in these various collaborative projects, the aforementioned scholars had gathered and analyzed the data and were able to display it in various ways. But at the end of the day (or more likely, at the end of the decade), here's what's important: as scholars, we assembled these data and synthesized our impressions and our numbers, in as powerful a way as we could. And over and above the data that we arrayed, we hoped that *our writings, individually or collectively, could change the conversation* about human beings at a particular time in a particular social and cultural context. I should point out the obvious: intent does not equal achievement. My collaborators and I have aimed to change the conversation; the other scholars I've mentioned succeeded in doing so.

Importantly, as scholars, our words, our terms, our concepts are intended to be *neutral*, or to use an adjective that is less familiar but more illuminating, we aspire to a *disinterested* stance. We attempt to describe a state of affairs as we have observed and analyzed it, not to prejudge or skew our findings and conclusions. But if we are successful, our very acts of conceptualization and writing may *change* how people talk and think. And, paradoxically, this very change may in the end—or, more precisely, in the next iteration—make our conceptualizations (as initially published) less accurate, less relevant, more like "period pieces" than the "last word."

A few examples: If we cast a spotlight on "bowling alone," perhaps people will start to bowl together. That will alter social relations in our time and, accordingly, we'll need a new way to talk about the emerging constellation of social relations. If we note the risks of "fast thinking," perhaps more of us will adopt slower thinking on more occasions, or maybe we'll come up with ways of oscillating among these alternative modes of thought. Perhaps if we describe identity crises carefully, fewer people will have them; or perhaps identity will play out differently for the "app generation." Indeed, that coauthored book represents a respectful critique both of David Riesman and colleagues (nowadays, we argue, young people are *app* directed, not *other* directed) and of Erik Erikson (identity formation may be more precocious or less solidified in a social media world; intimacy may be more elusive; imagination more likely to be collective).

You may well be thinking, "*This is not science*," at least not science as we know it or science as we heard it described in our school days. In one sense, science also changes—today we conceptualize atoms differently than did John Dalton, and genes differently than did William Bateson. But the atoms and genes *don't* change, nor do carbon molecules nor astro planets or geological strata (at least not quickly). What changes, on the bases of observations, experimentation, and critiques thereof, is how we name and describe these elements and how we assemble them together into larger schemes. If science is done well, it can be done anywhere by anyone who is trained, and in the end the conclusions should be roughly the same.

The state of affairs is *so different* in the realm of the mind, the culture, the society, that I think it is misleading to apply the same descriptor "science" to the aforementioned constructs.

So I no longer call what I do social science. If I had to choose a name, I could not think of a worse one than "Social Relations" or "Soc Rel"—founded in 1946, buried in 1972, may its name rest in peace! I'd like to sponsor a competition to come up with a better name. I actually like the phrases that I associate with social psychologist George Herbert Mead (Mind, Self, and Society) or with developmental psychologist Lev Vygotsky (Mind in Society). Interestingly, these phrases were created by editors of compilations, and not (so far as I know) by Mead or Vygotsky themselves. These somewhat noun-heavy phrases capture my long-term interest—indeed, my lifelong infatuation—with the human mind, along with the realization that minds develop and change within particular societies and cultures and that those macro-environments affect them powerfully, unpredictably, ceaselessly. Another candidate phrase would be "human studies"—but that phrase risks being transmogrified into humane or humanistic studies, neither of which I have in mind. "Person" lacks that baggage, but it seems a bit individualistic, so we could pluralize it to "Persons in Societies."

For now, given my fifty-plus years of fascination with the human mind, I'll describe it as "human syntheses about human minds." This formulation has the advantage that it denotes syntheses done by human beings (rather than primarily by computational devices, at least so far), and it is about human entities and activities. But it's wordy . . . so the raffle/competition/naming contest continues.

About twenty years ago, I had the pleasure of speaking to Murray Gell-Mann, Nobel Laureate in Physics in 1969 and the founding genius behind the interdisciplinary Santa Fe Institute. Almost as an aside, Gell-Mann said, "In the twenty-first century, the most important kind of mind will be the synthesizing mind."

Not only have I never forgotten this phrase, but in a 2005 book called *Five Minds for the Future*, with due credit to Gell-Mann, I wrote about the "synthesizing mind": the capacity to take in a lot of information, reflect on it, and then organize it in a way that is useful to you and (if you are skilled and fortunate) that also proves useful to others.

I am often asked about which intelligences I have and which I lack. I do my best to respond reflectively, as I did earlier in this memoir. But I've concluded that it's more useful, more informative, perhaps even more accurate to say that I have a *synthesizing mind*.

Accordingly, in what follows, I probe the synthesizing mind and offer my analysis of what it is and how it works (and, along the way, what it is not). I do so in two ways: (1) by contrasting synthesizing with the four other kinds of minds that I have described (disciplined, creative, respectful, ethical); and (2) by examining the act and skill of synthesizing via the lens of the multiple intelligences.

When introducing the five minds, I make two distinctions. First of all, these minds do not denote the kinds of scholarly distinctions made by psychologists about the operations of the human mind. In other words, I have not simply dropped three or four intelligences from the current list of eight or nine intelligences. Rather, they are characterizations, directed primarily at educators and policymakers, about the kinds of minds that we, and especially those of us who occupy positions as policymakers, should be cultivating in ourselves and nurturing in others in the years ahead. These are the kinds of minds we should be valuing both within and beyond formal school.

Second, two of the postulated five minds pertain to human beings living with others, both those near us (*the respectful mind*) and those with whom we have more remote contact (*the ethical mind*). My understanding of these two kinds of minds has emerged from our long-time and continuing study of good work, good play, good citizenships, and other kinds of' "goods" (see page 181). These minds are incredibly important for the survival as well as thriving of our

At its core, the *creating mind* solves problems or raises questions or introduces ideas or practices that are initially novel, if not unprecedented. But novelty alone is not enough—just thinking or doing "stuff" in an original way does not suffice. To be judged creative, an idea or practice must be *accepted in some way* by a relevant community. Put whimsically (or perhaps wistfully), it's not enough that your mother or father posts your finger-painting on the refrigerator door. The scribble or sketch has to capture the eye of the curator or the art critic or the writer of a textbook and/or the pocketbook of the collector, and eventually emerge as worthy of attention by other members of the public. And occasionally, the reverse process happens: for some reason, a run-of-the-mill action or product somehow goes viral and then the creator, critic, or collector takes note.

Now we come to the heart of the matter: *the line between synthesizing and creating.* It's hard to imagine *any* potentially creative idea or act being conjured up "from scratch." The ten years of disciplined training really matter. Even such indisputable prodigies as Mozart or Picasso in the arts, or indeed Bill Gates or Steve Jobs in computing, proceeded in workmanlike fashion in their chosen domain for years before achieving a creative breakthrough. So creativity presupposes both some disciplinary mastery and some prior synthesis.

But it is worth drawing a line—even a sharp line—between syntheses that are content to be syntheses and are accepted as such, and syntheses that aim for and may be accepted as creative by the relevant community. To use my own quite humble example: my textbook in social psychology (1970) is a mundane synthesis of major topics in the field and has had no appreciable impact on how social psychology is conceptualized or presented in subsequent texts. In contrast, my textbook in developmental psychology (1978;

second edition, 1982) is more innovative. It is organized by developmental stage rather than by topic (language development, social development, and so on); and it features interludes—short essays interspersed between chapters where I reflect on topics that happened to interest me (and, I hoped, students), rather than on topics already addressed by the research community or already on the radar screens of classroom teachers. And ultimately this textbook has had some impact on future texts in that field and, one would hope, on the ways in which students and teachers think about human development. Unlike my earlier text in social psychology, the developmental text gets at least modest marks for creativity.

Looking over my oeuvres of a lifetime, it is clear to me that most of my early works are primarily syntheses; two textbooks, my study of Piaget's and Lévi-Strauss's *Quest for Mind*, my survey of *The Shattered Mind*, and so on. I was displaying what the good and conscientious student has mastered. At its inception, the work on multiple intelligences was seen as a synthesis. In fact, as previously noted, it began with my initial intention of surveying different kinds of minds. But *Frames of Mind* moves significantly toward the pole of creativity in several ways:

it considered a far wider range of abilities than those usually considered by psychologists interested in cognition and intelligence;

it surveyed a far wider range of scholarly disciplines—from cultural studies to brain studies—than was typically the case;

it blurred the line between natural and social scientific research findings, on the one hand, and educational implications on the other; and, perhaps most prominently, if less predictably,

it pluralized and conferred new denotations and connotations on the venerable word "intelligence."

Possibly more than anything else that I'd written before or since, *Frames of Mind* is a synthesis that has changed the conversation about human intellect, particularly with reference to educational policy and practices. And more evocatively, it has catalyzed many individuals to think differently about themselves and about others—often persons to whom these individuals were close but whose minds had previously been mysterious, even opaque. And so it deserves a nod in the direction of creativity.

As I detail in *Five Minds for the Future*, syntheses can be adequate or inadequate, suited for one purpose or for a quite different one. But no matter the ambition or modesty of the synthesizer, he or she cannot simply *decide* or *declare* that a specific synthesis is also creative. That's a decision made only and appropriately by the wider community over the course of time. And so, as an example, Katie Davis and I hoped that young people in the twenty-first century would, following the examples of Riesman and Hochschild, come to be thought of as "the app generation." But that change in conceptualization and terminology has not happened yet and it probably never will. It fails the acid test for creativity.

A few more points about synthesizing. Some syntheses aim to bring lots of materials together to make a single grand point. We could call those "hedgehog" syntheses. Charles Darwin's *On the Origin of the Species* is an outstanding example. "Fox-like" syntheses delight in their plurality—Carl Jung's positing of various personality types might qualify. Some syntheses seek balance—Riesman's and Hochschild's portrayals of American life come to mind—while others push very hard in one direction or other—C. Wright Mills on the "power elite" and William Whyte on the "organization man" were both attempts to characterize American society in the 1950s.

And within the area of social analysis, some syntheses reflect great overarching concepts—the "grand theories" of Karl Marx, Max Weber, Sigmund Freud—whereas others are content to focus more deeply on a more manageable topic, what sociologist Robert Merton termed "theories of the middle range."

But by now, you may be posing the question that is most challenging for me to answer: is there a separate intelligence for synthesizing, or is the capacity that I am describing adequately explained by the operation of one or more of the several multiple intelligences?

Of course, everyone is free to claim or create the category of "synthesizing intelligence"; and I willingly concede that I sometimes have that bent or at least that aspiration. And I can readily cite authors who are expert synthesizers; I've mentioned paleontologist Stephen Jay Gould and geographer Jared Diamond, both of whom are also steeped in history and, as it happens, in music. Without stretching the point too far, I can talk of artists who also synthesize styles and formats. For example, after widely heralded creative breakthroughs in the opening decades of the twentieth century, composer Igor Stravinsky and his contemporary (and occasional collaborator) visual artist Pablo Picasso both went through a neo-classical period in the 1920s. As the name signals, both artists combined contemporary idioms with classical themes and forms. And some artists even deliberately synthesize media, such as opera composer Richard Wagner, with his *Gesamtkunstwerk*.[4]

---

4. This term denotes works that draw on several art forms in an effort to present a grand unified vision (or versions) of the world. It's also an apt characterization of artists who attempt to capture an entire universe. Consider the scope of the Inferno, Purgatory, and Paradise of Dante's *Divine Comedy*.

In contrast, some scholars, musicians, and painters are equally notable but explore the same topics and themes ever more deeply, rather than more widely or broadly. I think of a cognitive psychologist who has studied metaphoric and analogic thinking for forty years, or a neurobiologist who has focused for an equal length of time on a set of cells in the retina.

Still, as noted in my review of MI theory, I am very conservative with respect to conferring a seal of approval on any additional intelligences. I much prefer to construe the candidate skill in question as one that deploys two or more already "approved" intelligences in the cohort. For example, I have never been tempted to posit separate technological or digital intelligences. Such candidates are explained to my satisfaction by combinations of the already identified intelligences.

In a nutshell, here's my idea: Individuals can synthesize in various ways. How they do so depends on the intelligences that most characterize their own cognitive profile—the ones on which they most like to draw, and the ones most appropriate for the task at hand. Quite obviously, a composer like Stravinsky draws heavily on musical intelligence, while a painter like Picasso draws on his spatial and bodily intelligences. Such creative artists may well have strong linguistic and logical intelligences, but those "IQ" strengths are bonuses rather than requirements. As it happens, Stravinsky, trained as a lawyer, wrote prose that was sparkling and illuminating in several languages; in contrast, Picasso was a painting prodigy, and his writings and sayings are novelties, nothing more.

Synthesizers like the aforementioned Gould or Diamond (and I could conjure up numerous names across the spectrum of scholarly disciplines) naturally draw on the intelligences that scholars use, and so both of them presumably have abundant linguistic and logical intelligences. But they probably have more developed linguistic intelligences than, say, Murray Gell-Mann, the coiner of the term "synthesizing mind," who signed a contract to write a book but had enormous difficulty in completing it. In contrast, many brilliant physicists, mathematicians, and computer scientists would rather tinker than talk, never have any urge to write out what they have been thinking in more than a few pages, or prefer mathematical symbols to linguistic tropes. I began to write regularly, if not compulsively, as soon as I could hold a pencil or type on a keyboard or place letters on a platen; over the decades I have rarely searched for numerical signs or symbols, let alone felt any urge to create new ones.

So far my descriptions, though admittedly based simply on biographical information and not on "tests," seem plausible. It would be hard, if not perverse, to state that dancer Martha Graham lacked bodily intelligence or that physicist Marie Curie lacked logical-mathematical intelligence. Indeed, if psychological tests were to challenge those characterizations, I would question the validity of those tests.

But I suspect that those of us who are synthesizers also draw on our other less obvious intelligences in ways that prove helpful to us and perhaps to others. For example, as a physicist Einstein would probably be seen as a prototypical master of logical-mathematical intelligence. Yet he actually had a highly developed spatial intelligence, while he needed the help of his friend Marcel Grossmann to execute the mathematics appropriate for the general (as compared to the special) theory of relativity. As a scientist and physician, Freud had adequate logical and spatial intelligence, but he really stood out for his linguistic skills; in 1930 he won the prestigious Goethe Prize for literary excellence.

Since I am indulging in the just-contrived parlor game of analyzing synthesizers in terms of their most helpful intelligences ("name the intelligences of synthesizing"), let me peer into my own MI mirror. As I stated in earlier chapter, my linguistic intelligence is fine, and my logical skills are certainly adequate. As for interpersonal intelligence, this should be a requirement for psychologists, at least those who study or seek to help human beings.

But as I consider my own methods for synthesizing, I have come up with a somewhat different analysis. As a synthesizer, I believe that I draw on two other intelligences. First of all, as one deeply involved in music since early childhood, I think of writing, and particularly the writing of a book, as if it were the creation of a symphonic composition, with movements, themes, anticipations, recapitulations, interludes, and the like. Both with respect to my own writing and that of students and colleagues, from early on, I have an overall sense of the form and structure of the final piece; and in my case I like to pound out a detailed outline or even a whole draft early on. I have a developed sense of the order in which themes should be introduced; when various "instruments" should be foregrounded; the implications of moving a text or a point to a different spot in the literary tapestry, or of expanding or eliminating it; what serves as an overture, the development of a theme, a climax and conclusion, even a coda (stay tuned!). Perhaps I am fooling myself that I do this effectively, but I believe that I *do* do it, and I strive to do it reasonably well.

The other perhaps surprising intelligence on which I draw is that of the naturalist. In truth, I don't have much interest in the natural outdoors—despite spending all those years at summer camp and passing all of the relevant merit badges needed to become an Eagle Scout. But as I try to make sense of all that I have seen, heard, read, and thought, I am constantly coming up with schemes, ways of classifying and reclassifying, tables, simple images, orderings and reorderings. To be sure, this is hardly in the league of naturalists like Linnaeus or Darwin or Audubon, but it represents a legitimate effort to make optimal sense of the variety of "species" that I have collected. And that may be why I have always been far more attracted to biology than to the other physical or natural sciences, and why I enjoyed my years working as a neurologist "from the neck up." That said, I suspect I would have been a more successful biologist in the nineteenth or early twentieth century than in the current era, where mathematics and computing are increasingly important, and classifying is more likely to be done by a computer program or deep learning algorithm than by a human eye and a human brain.

Of course, all of this is self-analysis. And, if I can poke fun at my arsenal of intelligences, the truth of it depends on whether I have keen intrapersonal intelligence. But as I think about synthesizing more broadly, beyond my own perhaps peculiar personal psychology, I propose a few additional points.

First of all, synthesizing involves artistry. To create a work or treatment of significant size and to convey it effectively to others requires a sense of form, of arrangement of parts, of the attention and predilection of audiences, of launching, development, and closure. All of these skills are identified particularly with the arts more so than with the sciences, where the behavior and accurate description of reality has to take primacy. I propose that synthesizers are aspiring artists, and that they—and that includes me—draw from the art form with which they are most comfortable—be it musical, literary, architectural, terpsichorean, or some other aesthetic means of communication.

But unlike "pure" artists, synthesizers cannot start from scratch and proceed in any and all directions. Rather, they are restricted, or if you prefer empowered, by the data that they and others have collected, be it historical, literary, or psychological. And accordingly, these aspiring synthesizers need some ways to arrange and rearrange those data, until they find a solution that is adequate, accurate, communicable, and, as a bonus, aesthetically pleasing. In my case, I proceed in the ways of a naturalist, labeling and relabeling different species of data. But I suspect that there are many ways of ordering and reordering—perhaps even as many as there are synthesizers or at least types of synthesizers.

I am prepared to go further. Just as individuals draw on their favored intelligences in mastering schoolwork or in creating new works, so, too, those of us who are engaged in synthesizing are inclined to exploit those intelligences which we favor, and which help us to make sense of our experiences. Think of the intelligences as a chart of chemical elements: aspiring synthesizers create the particular configuration of chemical compounds that allow them to carry out their mission.

As I pointed out in *Five Minds for the Future*, psychology has largely dropped the ball with respect to illumination of this form of cognition. We have little understanding of how we humans synthesize information and then collate it in ways that are helpful to us and to others, and in ways that are either adequate, fine, outstanding, or truly creative. This skill does not lend itself to examination via simple laboratory experiments and concomitant rapid publication in highly ranked peer-reviewed journals; hence the pau-city of relevant research on the kind of broad synthesizing that I am describing. This state of affairs constitutes an inviting challenge for students who enjoy synthesizing, and who may be able to illumi-nate its operations, at least until such time as a master "deep learn-ing" algorithm renders anachronistic the synthesizing intelligences as practiced heretofore by human beings.

My own case study here provides possible starting points for such an enterprise. A future student or scholar of synthesis might carry out comparisons at a certain moment in time: the rise, breadth, and reasons for curiosity in early childhood (for example, what it means to grow up in a household where important information has been concealed and where so much of the ambient society is unfamiliar to the adults—who grew up elsewhere); the ways in which a motley collection of information is stored and retained in the absence of intellectual coat-racks; the extent to which those packets of information are linked or allowed to float in cognitive space; the impulse to record tentative syntheses, in an appropriate symbolic form; the urge to put together disparate bodies and forms of information; the tendency to master, dabble in, challenge, or cir-cumvent existing disciplines; the stretch (or nonstretch) to creativity (for example, whether one is talking about classroom assignments or dissertations, the production of reliable summaries as opposed to the search for ambitious breakthroughs); as well as the diffi-cult decision of what to leave out, or to postpone for another day or another publication. Or such a student of synthesis might carry out longitudinal case studies of individuals with clear synthesizing gifts, and compare them with one another, or, indeed, with equally talented individuals who are perhaps outstanding disciplinarians or creators, but display no particular inclinations or gifts in synthesizing or whose syntheses are decidedly modest, misleading, or even useless. (I've fantasized about a study of four individuals nicknamed Steve—geologist Gould, physicist Weinberg, psychologist Pinker, literary scholar Greenblatt—probing how each of them has become a master of synthesis.)

Then there is the question of "educating for synthesizing." As already noted, we make modest requests for synthesizing when we ask students to write book reports or carry out a project or produce an essay in response to a probe on a test. There are criteria for judging these productions (ones that our students push for nowadays if we teachers don't lay out the rules for rendering such judgments, preferably in excruciating detail). Schoolwork beyond these modest requirements is generally a term paper or a thesis in a discipline, where the student is expected in some way to stretch beyond the existing literature or already secured experimental results. If, indeed, the synthesizing mind is important in our time, it seems well worth efforts to develop it systematically and skillfully.

In deciphering how to navigate large bodies of knowledge, especially knowledge drawn from disparate disciplines, and how to do so in a way that is effective and that moves the conversation along, even if it does not change it, scholars are largely on their own. There are remarkably few guides. And so, as in my case, aspiring synthesizers have to depend on role models. I was fortunate to have had both synthesizers whom I knew personally, like psychologist Jerome Bruner and sociologist David Riesman, and so-called paragons (individuals whom one admires from afar), like historian Richard Hofstadter and essayist Edmund Wilson. And we aspiring synthesizers must draw on our peculiar motivations and skills and intelligences, such as they are and such as they can be cultivated or even synthesized.

But in the future, there's no need for budding synthesizers to proceed on their own. Even to introduce the "word" and the "concept" of "synthesizing" in school would be a positive step. Instructors can model how they go about making sense of disparate data—as I have often done with my students, both in a classroom setting and in one-on-one conversations with doctoral students. One can study the syntheses that we admire and that are useful to us, as well as those that are confusing or that leave us uninspired (comparing how different textbooks cover the same topic can be enlightening). And most important, one can explicitly assign "challenges of synthesis" to students, ask for their planned approach, provide feedback on these "specs," look at drafts and provide further feedback, then have students read or examine the efforts to their classmates and indicate where they inspire and where they fall short. Indeed, such procedures are often followed with respect to lab reports or book reports or, more ambitiously, to term papers or theses—what I'm calling for is a *much more explicit concern* with what makes for an effective synthesis and the various ways in which such synthesis can fall wide of the mark.

While I have focused on school-based, written syntheses, the same general process can be followed with respect to many other forms of synthesizing. As already mentioned, many artists carry out synthesizing in the symbol systems favored by their art form. And without stretching the concept unduly, synthesizing occurs across many domains of practice. Think of the judge who has to make a decision about a complex case and then issue a decision; the physician who has to cull all sorts of tests and observations and come up with the most likely diagnosis; the curator or the city planner who has to mount an exhibition or a celebratory event; the corporate leader who decides to create a new business plan; or the management consultant charged with providing useful feedback to an enterprise that has foundered. One could write a book about "varieties of syntheses" and "varieties of synthesizers."

A final word about synthesizing. The kinds of synthesizing on which I have focused in these pages might be called large-scale synthesizing, the sort that scholars undertake and that is found in books, summary articles, or major artistic or design endeavors. But we also live in an era where rewards come to those who can synthesize in a versatile way: provide a brief summary of a complex set of ideas; write a blog; give a TED talk; do an effective interview on radio, TV, or a podcast; create a stimulating tweet and marvel if it goes viral.

But—an important "but"—can such a quick and necessarily superficial synthesizer go deeper, provide more details, handle challenges, realize when a criticism is valid as opposed to being irrelevant or based on a fundamental misunderstanding? Only if the answer to these questions is "yes" would I deem such a person to be a legitimate synthesizer. Indeed, with respect to my theory of multiple intelligences, I have seen and heard literally hundreds of superficial syntheses of the theory. The ones that I value are the ones put forth by individuals who have taken the trouble to read my writings, discuss and debate them with others (including me), ponder the implications, and provide answers and critiques that are thoughtful rather than thoughtless. A trenchant critique of a synthesis may well itself depend on a synthesizing mind.

Murray Gell-Mann spoke about the synthesizing mind as central in our century, and I believe that he was correct. But this claim raises the issue of whether it will continue to be important thereafter, and if so, whether the synthesizing be done by human beings, by artificial intelligence, or by some combination of protoplasmic and "chip" machinery. I lack expertise or even strong intuitions in this area. To be sure, I have no doubt that aspiring synthesizers will appreciate and make use of the most powerful and most appropriate computational devices and resources. As a modest example, in the Good Work project in the 1990s, we did most of our analyses by reading and coding and applying a few statistical tests. In contrast, in our study of higher education two decades later, we are using "big data" programs to analyze the words and phrases used by two thousand constituents across several campuses.

But computational approaches will also stretch us in unanticipated directions. As just one example, most individuals today are trained in specific disciplines or forms of expertise and draw on the tools of their respective disciplines. In contrast, "deep learning" algorithms simply process data without such classificatory bins, unless they are so "primed." Such "undisciplined" minds may reveal patterns and interactions that would otherwise have been missed. Someone might even create a "Howard Gardner synthesizing app" that synthesizes in the way that I would have, but does a better job than I could have. In which case I really could retire!

Personally, I am unenthusiastic about allowing computational devices to determine *which* questions should be asked, to dictate *what* should be synthesized, to judge *whether* the particular synthesis is appropriate for the task and the user, and to decide *how* the results should be interpreted. Nor am I by any means ready to turn over moral or ethical decisions to an algorithm, no matter how intelligent or even "multiply intelligent" it is declared to be! However, there are likely to be goals and processes of synthesizing à la AI that are difficult even to envision at this point, at least by me.

From early on I have been disposed to ask questions, to reflect about them, to gather whatever data are available by whatever means I have at my disposal, and then, crucially, to organize those data in ways that made sense to me, and, I hope, to others as well. Thanks to the accidents of family, culture, the historical moment, and, yes, genes, I have had the privilege of being able to lead a life of the mind, and to put forth syntheses that make sense to me, and, at least at times, to others as well. I have done this chiefly through writing books, though as other media have become available or salient, I've been able to draw on them as well. And if I continue to be fortunate, I'll be able to continue to do this for a while, and to support others—students near and mentees far and correspondents wherever—who seek to do the same. Indeed, there is an apparent advantage to the synthesizing impulse, which I had not certainly not anticipated when I was younger. As one ages, and one's memory for names or appointments or the location of car keys declines, the impulse and even the capacity for synthesizing seems to remain intact. One might even call it wisdom.

Perhaps, as I say, such syntheses will be done ably by the techniques and the technologies of artificial intelligence. But I don't readily foresee individuals like David Riesman, Erik Erikson, Margaret Mead or Arlie Hochschild (or the aforementioned four persons named Steven or Stephen) becoming anachronistic. And that's because the synthesis depends crucially on *the quality of the questions asked and on the reasons that they are being asked.* Only then can the synthesizer (whether flesh-and-blood or silicon) identify the relevant pieces, arrange and rearrange them, and ultimately configure them in a presentation that makes sense to the creator and, if fortunate, to others as well.

Whether I occupy even a modest place in that star-studded array of synthesizers is not for me to judge.

Before wrapping up, I want to return to my student who asked how I felt about the discovery for which I am likely to be known. I have no regrets about developing the theory of multiple intelligences or writing *Frames of Mind*. The benefits for me have been plentiful, and I am confident enough to assert that they have also been beneficial to many others in many situations around the world. As for any damage done, I regret this very much. I wish that I could have done more to prevent it.

Nor do I regret the timing. Prior to the publication of *Frames of Mind*, I had fifteen years of preparation in psychology and other natural and social sciences that enabled me to carry out that work of synthesis. And thereafter, I have had the luxury of pondering further implications, without letting myself be overburdened by the "MI responsibility" unless I have so chosen. And as a scholar in a country and at a time when there were no "thought police," I have had the opportunity to follow up issues that interested me, to synthesize my "data'" in ways that made sense to me, and to write them up in appropriate formats.

Regarding lessons for others, I will limit myself to a few closing comments.

First of all, should you have the privilege of changing the conversation, be grateful. Don't assume that you can control the ensuing conversation—you will in all likelihood fail—but you do have a responsibility to help guide it in productive ways. And if synthesizing in the area of human minds and human activities is appealing, go for it. Perhaps you will even be able to explain how the synthesizing mind develops and how it operates in full throttle.

Second, try to explain your enterprise to others in the most suitable terms and concepts. For too long, I thought that I had to justify my work in terms of "harder" disciplines, be it logic and mathematics on the one hand, or on biology, neurology, and genetics on the other. I don't think that such strained rationales are necessary or wise. Rather, try as best you can to describe just what you have done, with what evidence and analytic tools you have, while indicating as well what you have not done and what you are not able to do.

And don't assume that others will know what you are doing or why you have done it, unless you can explain it clearly and, if necessary, repeatedly and in different yet appropriate ways.

In my case, I have not done journalism, nor have I done science, with a capital S. Focusing on human cognition in human societies, I have sought to carry out syntheses that are useful; to indicate how I have done them; if fortunate, to affect or even change the conversation, and to be open to that change bringing about yet other changes, which we might not have anticipated but which we can, if we so choose, then critique, evaluate, and build on.

The cycle continues.

May the human conversation—better, the human conversations—also continue. "May synthesizing minds thrive."

ACKNOWLEDGMENTS

I've written many books, but memoirs—even intellectual ones—are different. I've had a lot of helpful advice and feedback from many individuals.

At the MIT Press, I thank my editor Susan Buckley, who spent much time thinking with me about how best to present both old ideas and new ones, how to mix the personal and the professional; her associate Noah Springer; Judith Feldmann, an excellent copy editor whose speed and accuracy are admirable; and Amy Brand and Gita Manaktala, for their support of this project. As has been the case for many active and pleasurable decades, the agent team of Ike Williams and Hope Denekamp were available whenever I needed their counsel.

Many friends were kind enough to read earlier versions of this memoir and to offer helpful feedback. I thank Joe Blatt, Anne Colby, Bill Damon, Tom Dingman, Susan Engel, Wendy Fischman,

Marion Gardner-Saxe, Eldon Greenberg, Stephen Greenblatt, Andy Hargreaves, Ben Heineman, Tom Hoerr, Mia Keinanen, Mindy Kornhaber, Yael Karakowsky, Ashley Lee, Konstantin Offer, Len Saxe, Henry Timms, and Stanton Wortham. My wife, Ellen, provided constant support as well as her customary shrewd editorial comments and suggestions.

My wonderful office team handled all of the aspects that I could not deal with myself. Special appreciation to Courtney Bither, Shinri Furuzawa, Danny Mucinskas, and Jordan Pickard. Courtney also prepared the index deftly, carefully, and expeditiously.

My greatest debt is to the individuals to whom I express appreciation on the dedication page of the book. And I want to conclude with special gratitude to members of my immediate family who accepted my decision to reflect on my life and gave candid and useful feedback along the way. Except for August-Pierre, who arrived after the photograph was taken, you can see them all in the 2019 snapshot, included in the second set of photos.

APPENDIX: LIST OF BLOG POSTS BY THE AUTHOR

Reverse Chronological List of Blogs on Multiple Intelligences Written or Curated by Howard Gardner

1.	"My Thoughts on 'Emotional Intelligence'"	December 18, 2019
2.	"The Ranking of U.S. States by Intelligence"	December 9, 2019
3.	"How Dance Helps Children with Special Needs"	November 25, 2019
4.	"How to Teach History Using MI Theory"	October 1, 2019
5.	"Why Learning Styles Based on Sensory Organs Make No Sense"	September 5, 2019
6.	"Where Is Talent?"	August 15, 2019
7.	"An Interview with Long Term Economy"	August 7, 2019
8.	"An Interview on Children and Multiple Intelligences"	July 16, 2019
9.	"Trump and IQ"	June 17, 2019
10.	"Do Highly Intelligent People Prefer Instrumental Music?"	June 5, 2019

11.	"Interview by the National Art Education Association"	May 21, 2019
12.	"MI Misconceptions: An Article from Pakistan"	May 3, 2019
13.	"Article on Intelligence Ignores MI Theory"	April 18, 2019
14.	"How Can I Build an MI Test? "	March 19, 2019
15.	"Q&A with Students around the World"	February 5, 2019
16.	"Existential Intelligence in Gifted Children"	January 7, 2019
17.	"Game-Based Learning Program Helps Kids Find Their Dream Job"	September 26, 2018
18.	"What Should Be in an MI Library? An MI Expert Explains"	September 6, 2018
19.	"*Harvard Gazette* Interview"	May 15, 2018
20.	"MI after 35 Years"	May 2, 2018
21.	"Podcast: Discussing MI Theory with Alanis Morissette"	March 15, 2018
22.	"Study Finds Game-Based Learning Can Increase Intelligences in Students"	February 13, 2018
23.	"Naturalist Intelligence in the Age of the iPhone"	January 31, 2018
24.	"A New Possibility for Musical Intelligence"	January 8, 2018
25.	"Audi Piloted Driving Show Car Uses '8 Intelligences'"	December 19, 2017
26.	"An MI Science Lesson to Emulate"	December 8, 2017
27.	"Contrasting Views of Human Behavior and Human Mind: An Epistemological Drama in Five Acts"	November 14, 2017
28.	"Comment on 'Three Cognitive Dimensions for Tracking Deep Learning Progress'"	October 31, 2017
29.	"MI Perspective on General Intelligence"	August 23, 2017
30.	"Study of Spatial Intelligence"	July 12, 2017
31.	"New Children's Book about MI Theory"	June 28, 2017
32.	"Three Messages from the 'MI Front'"	May 31, 2017

33.	"Could 'Green' Hospitals Encourage Naturalist Intelligence in Children?"	April 20, 2017
34.	"Study of Learning Disorders: Evidence for MI Theory?"	March 24, 2017
35.	"MI and Habits of Mind in Arts Education"	March 10, 2017
36.	"MI and Law Enforcement"	February 9, 2017
37.	"Guest Blog Series: MI Intelligences in Music"	January 25, 2017
38.	"Interview with Tiching Blog"	December 7, 2016
39.	"The Neuroscience of Intelligences"	November 2, 2016
40.	"Specialization in the SAT: The Math Portion Should Only Test Math Skills"	October 6, 2016
41.	"Proposal to Integrate Music and Math Education"	September 22, 2016
42.	"Multiple Intelligences Featured by French Education Site"	August 10, 2016
43.	"The Man Who Wasn't There"	June 24, 2016
44.	"Howard Gardner Speaks at Arizona State University"	June 8, 2016
45.	"SPARK Memories Radio and its Implications for MI"	May 25, 2016
46.	"Dr. Marty Nemko of Psychology Today Interviews Howard Gardner"	April 28, 2016
47.	"Multiple Intelligence International School Celebrates 20 Years"	April 12, 2016
48.	"Howard Gardner Discusses Standardized Testing in Interview with Big Think"	March 29, 2016
49.	"New Research Supports Existence of a Music Center in the Brain"	March 2, 2016
50.	"Interview by Esther Cepeda Regarding Learning Styles"	February 16, 2016
51.	"Article Regarding Standardized Testing and Inequality in Schools"	January 7, 2016
52.	"Is the Brain a Computer?"	December 8, 2015

BIBLIOGRAPHY

Chen, Jie-Qi, Seana Moran, and Howard Gardner, eds. *Multiple Intelligences around the World.* San Francisco, CA: Jossey Bass, 2009.

Erikson, Erik H. *Childhood and Society.* New York: Norton, 1950.

Fodor, Jerry. *The Modularity of Mind: An Essay on Faculty Psychology.* Cambridge, MA: MIT Press, 1983.

Gardner, Howard. *Art, Mind, and Brain: A Cognitive Approach to Creativity.* New York: Basic Books, 1982.

Gardner, Howard. *Artful Scribbles: The Significance of Children's Drawings.* New York: Basic Books, 1980.

Gardner, Howard. *The Arts and Human Development.* New York: Wiley, 1973.

Gardner, Howard. *Creating Minds: An Anatomy of Creativity Seen through the Lives of Freud, Einstein, Picasso, Stravinsky, Eliot, Graham, and Gandhi.* New York: Basic Books, 1993.

Gardner, Howard. *Developmental Psychology: An Introduction*. Boston: Little, Brown, 1978.

Gardner, Howard. *The Disciplined Mind: What All Students Should Understand*. New York: Simon & Schuster, 1999.

Gardner, Howard. *Five Minds for the Future*. Boston: Harvard Business School Press, 2007.

Gardner, Howard. *Frames of Mind: The Theory of Multiple Intelligences*. New York: Basic Books, 1983/2011.

Gardner, Howard. *The Mind's New Science: A History of the Cognitive Revolution*. New York: Knopf, 1985.

Gardner, Howard. *Multiple Intelligences: New Horizons*. New York: Basic Books, 2006.

Gardner, Howard. *The Quest for Mind: Jean Piaget, Claude Lévi-Strauss, and the Structuralist Movement*. New York: Knopf, 1973/1981.

Gardner, Howard. "Reflections on Multiple Intelligences: Myths and Messages." *Phi Delta Kappan* 77, no. 3 (Nov. 1995): 200–209.

Gardner, Howard. *The Shattered Mind: The Person after Brain Damage*. New York: Knopf, 1975.

Gardner, Howard. "The Synthesizing Mind: Making Sense of the Deluge of Information." In *Globalization and Education*, ed. M. Sanchez-Sorondo et al., 3–18. New York: Walter de Gruyter, 2007.

Gardner, Howard. *Truth, Beauty, and Goodness Reframed: Educating for the Virtues in the Era of Truthiness and Twitter*. New York: Basic Books, 2011.

Gardner, Howard. *The Unschooled Mind: How Children Think and How Schools Should Teach*. New York: Basic Books, 1991.

Gardner, Howard, Mihaly Csikszentmihalyi, and William Damon. *Good Work: When Excellence and Ethics Meet*. New York: Basic Books, 2001.

Gardner, Howard, and Katie Davis. *The App Generation: How Today's Youth Navigate Identity, Intimacy, and Imagination in a Digital World*. New Haven, CT: Yale University Press, 2013.

Gardner, Howard, with Emma Laskin. *Leading Minds: An Anatomy of Leadership*. New York: Basic Books, 1995.

Goldman, Eric F. *Rendezvous with Destiny: A History of Modern American Reform*. New York: Vintage Books, 1953.

Goleman, Daniel. *Emotional Intelligence: Why It Can Matter More Than IQ*. New York: Bantam Books, 1995.

Goodman, Nelson. *Languages of Art: An Approach to a Theory of Symbols*. Indianapolis: Hackett, 1968.

Grossack, Martin M., and Howard Gardner. *Man and Men: Social Psychology as Social Science*. Scranton, PA: International Textbook, 1970.

Hochschild, Arlie Russell. *Strangers in Their Own Land: Anger and Mourning on the American Right*. New York: The New Press, 2016.

Hofstadter, Richard. *The American Political Tradition and the Men Who Made It*. New York: Knopf, 1948.

Jameson, J. Franklin. *The American Revolution Considered as a Social Movement*. Princeton, NJ: Princeton University Press, 1926.

Kahneman, Daniel. *Thinking Fast and Slow*. New York: Farrar, Straus and Giroux, 2011.

Lévi-Strauss, Claude. *Structural Anthropology*. New York: Basic Books, 1963.

National Commission on Excellence in Education. *A Nation at Risk: The Imperative for Educational Reform*. April 1983.

Piaget, Jean. "Piaget's Theory." In *Handbook of Child Psychology*, ed. P. Mussen. Hoboken, NJ: John Wiley & Sons, 1970.

Putnam, Robert D. *Bowling Alone: The Collapse and Revival of American Community.* New York: Simon & Schuster, 2000.

Riesman, David, with Nathan Glazer and Reuel Denny. *The Lonely Crowd: A Study of the Changing American Character.* New Haven, CT: Yale University Press, 1950.

Salovey, Peter, and John D. Mayer. "Emotional Intelligence." *Imagination, Cognition, and Personality* 9 (1990): 185–211.

Schaler, Jeffrey A. *Howard Gardner Under Fire.* Chicago: Open Court, 2006.

Sternberg, Robert J. *Beyond IQ: A Triarchic Theory of Human Intelligence.* New York: Cambridge University Press, 1985.

Thorn, Frederick Charles. *Principles of Psychological Examining: A Systematic Textbook of Applied Integrative Psychology.* Brandon, VT: Journal of Clinical Psychology, 1955.

Vance, J. D. *Hillbilly Elegy.* New York: Harper, 2016.

Wilson, Edmund. *Axel's Castle: A Study in the Imaginative Literature of 1870–1930.* Wailegam, IL: Fontana, 1931.

Wilson, Edmund. *To the Finland Station: A Study in the Writing and Acting of History.* New York: Harcourt, 1940.

Winner, Ellen. *How Art Works.* New York: Oxford University Press, 2018.

Winner, Ellen. *Invented Worlds.* Cambridge, MA: Harvard University Press, 1982.

Winner, Ellen, and Howard Gardner. "The Comprehension of Metaphor in Brain-Damaged Patients." *Brain* 100 (1977): 719–727.

INDEX